BRAINWAVES FOR GAMERS

A Step-by-Step Guide to Enhancing Your Focus, Speed, Reaction Time, and Mind-Controlled Gaming

Dr. Niloufar Sarraf

Copyright © 2024 Dr. Niloufar Sarraf

All rights reserved

The characters and events portrayed in this book are fictitious. Any similarity to real persons, living or dead, is coincidental and not intended by the author.

No part of this book may be reproduced, or stored in a retrieval system, or transmitted in any form or by any means, electronic, mechanical, photocopying, recording, or otherwise, without express written permission of the publisher.

ISBN-13: 9798304340700
ISBN-10: Independently published

Cover design by: Art Painter
Library of Congress Control Number: 2018675309
Printed in the United States of America

CONTENTS

Title Page

Copyright

Preface

Chapter 1: Mastering Focus and Performance with EEG   1

Chapter 2: Exploring BCI Gaming – Playing Games with Your Brain   33

Chapter 3: The Future of Gaming with EEG   65

Chapter 4: Opportunities to Monetize EEG and Gaming Innovations   78

Conclusion   88

Appendix   90

About The Author   95

Books By This Author   97

PREFACE

The human brain is a marvel of nature—an intricate network of electrical signals, thoughts, and emotions that governs how we perceive and interact with the world. As someone who has spent years studying and researching brainwave dynamics, I remain fascinated by the untapped potential of harnessing these signals for personal growth, enhanced focus, and innovation.

In my previous book, Harnessing Brainwaves for Better Living and Success, I explored how understanding and leveraging brainwaves can empower individuals to achieve their goals and transform their lives. That work focused on personal growth, productivity, and mental wellness. Now, with Brainwaves for Gamers, I am thrilled to take this journey into the vibrant and fast-evolving world of gaming.

With a PhD in Neuro Information Science, I have always been driven by the intersection of neuroscience and technology. EEG technology, which allows us to observe and utilize brainwave patterns, is more than just a tool for research—it's a gateway to unlocking new ways of thinking, creating, and connecting. Nowhere is this more evident than in the gaming industry, where EEG offers unprecedented opportunities for immersion, focus, and innovation.

This book is a call to action for gamers, developers, and

innovators. It delves into the practical applications of EEG for mastering focus and performance, explores the possibilities of playing games with your mind, and takes a glimpse into the future of gaming powered by brainwaves. It also uncovers the exciting potential for monetization and entrepreneurial ventures in this emerging field.

Brainwaves for Gamers is more than just a guide; it's an invitation to think differently about the relationship between mind and machine, and to envision a future where the boundaries of gaming are limited only by our imagination. Whether you're a seasoned gamer or simply curious about the intersection of neuroscience and technology, I hope this book inspires you to explore the possibilities that lie ahead.

Welcome to the next level of gaming—powered by your mind.

CHAPTER 1: MASTERING FOCUS AND PERFORMANCE WITH EEG

In the fast-paced world of gaming, focus and precision are everything. Whether you're a casual gamer or a competitive esports athlete, the ability to concentrate deeply and react swiftly can make all the difference. Chapter 1 sets the foundation for understanding how EEG technology can unlock your peak gaming performance. By tapping into the natural rhythms of your brainwaves, you'll discover practical ways to enhance focus, improve reaction times, and maintain mental clarity during even the most challenging gameplay.

In this chapter, we'll delve into the science of brainwaves and their role in gaming, guiding you through the basics of measuring and interpreting your neural activity. From practical exercises to analyze your own brainwaves to tips for building a sustainable routine, this chapter equips you with the tools to achieve a competitive edge. Whether you're seeking to dominate in a high-stakes tournament or simply level up your personal gaming skills, EEG-driven techniques offer a new and powerful approach to mastering focus and performance.

1.1 Introduction to EEG in Gaming Performance

Welcome to the first part of EEG for Gamers! In this section, we'll explore how EEG (Electroencephalography) can help you take your gaming skills to the next level. Whether you're a competitive eSports player or a casual gamer, understanding and training your brainwaves can give you a serious edge.

What is EEG and Why Does it Matter for Gamers?

EEG is a non-invasive technique that measures electrical activity in your brain. This activity is represented as brainwaves—patterns of neural signals that reflect your mental states like focus, relaxation, and stress. For gamers, these mental states can determine your:

- Focus: Your ability to concentrate on the game and ignore distractions.
- Reaction Time: How quickly you respond to visual or auditory cues.
- Decision-Making: Staying sharp during critical moments in gameplay.
- Stress Resilience: Managing pressure in high-stakes matches.

Using EEG, you can measure, understand, and train your brainwaves to optimize these key areas, ultimately improving your performance and gaming experience.

Why Brainwaves Matter in Competitive and Casual Gaming

Whether you're competing in an eSports tournament or just playing for fun, your brain plays a huge role in determining your success.

- Competitive Gamers: Precision focus and stress management are essential to outperform your opponents. EEG can help you train your brain to enter a state of "flow," where you're

fully immersed and performing at your peak.
- Casual Gamers: EEG tools can enhance relaxation and enjoyment, helping you manage frustration and stay focused on achieving your in-game goals.

What You'll Learn in This Part
This part of the book is your roadmap to using EEG for gaming performance. We'll cover:

1. Understanding brainwaves and their connection to focus, flow, and stress.
2. How to measure and interpret your brainwaves using affordable EEG devices.
3. Practical exercises to train your brain for better focus, reaction time, and stress management.
4. Real-world examples of how gamers have used EEG to improve their gameplay.
5. Tips for building a daily or weekly EEG routine to track and enhance your performance.

By the end of this section, you'll have a solid foundation for using EEG as a tool to boost your focus, sharpen your decision-making, and stay calm under pressure—all skills that can give you the competitive edge you're looking for.

1.2 Understanding Brainwaves for Gaming

To unlock the full potential of EEG (brainwaves) for improving your gaming performance, it's essential to understand the brainwaves you'll be working with. Each brainwave reflects a different mental state, and knowing how to influence these states can help you stay sharp, focused, and relaxed when gaming.

Understanding Brainwaves: A Deeper Dive
Brainwaves are the electrical activity generated by neurons communicating with each other in the brain. These electrical signals are measurable using Electroencephalography (EEG), a technique that has paved the way for understanding the dynamic

nature of our brain's activity.

What Are Brainwaves?

At the core of brain function lies electrical signaling. Neurons, the building blocks of the brain, generate tiny electrical impulses as they send and receive information. These impulses create oscillations—rhythmic patterns of electrical activity—that flow across the brain, which we refer to as brainwaves. Brainwaves are categorized based on their frequency, measured in Hertz (Hz), or cycles per second.

- High-frequency waves are associated with focus, alertness, and cognitive tasks.
- Low-frequency waves emerge during relaxation, meditation, and sleep states.

EEG is the primary tool for measuring brainwaves, allowing scientists, doctors, and now individuals like you to observe and understand this hidden communication within the brain.

The Historical Context of Brainwaves

The discovery of brainwaves began in the early twentieth century. In 1924, German psychiatrist Hans Berger successfully recorded the first EEG, revolutionizing neuroscience. Berger observed the alpha waves, a type of brainwave associated with a relaxed, wakeful state. This groundbreaking discovery confirmed that the brain produces measurable electrical activity, leading to decades of research into brainwave patterns and their implications for health, behavior, and performance.

Through the years, EEG technology advanced significantly, making it accessible not just to researchers and clinicians but also to hobbyists, students, and gamers. Today, commercial EEG devices like Emotiv and Muse have unlocked the ability to harness brainwave data for personal growth, focus, and gaming.

The Five Types of Brainwaves

Brainwaves are divided into five primary categories, each serving a unique function in our mental states:

1. Delta Waves (0.5–4 Hz):
   a. The slowest brainwaves.
   b. Linked to deep sleep, healing, and restorative processes.
2. Theta Waves (4–8 Hz):
   a. Associated with light sleep, meditation, and creativity.
   b. Often observed during "in the zone" moments when the mind wanders or daydreams.
3. Alpha Waves (8–13 Hz):
   a. Present during calm, relaxed states while awake.
   b. Linked to mental clarity and readiness, commonly observed when closing your eyes and relaxing.
4. Beta Waves (13–30 Hz):
   a. Reflect active thinking, problem-solving, and focus.
   b. High beta levels can also correlate with stress and anxiety when overactive.
5. Gamma Waves (30–100 Hz):
   a. The fastest brainwaves, associated with heightened mental activity and peak cognitive performance.
   b. Linked to learning, problem-solving, and complex thought processes.

Why Brainwaves Matter for Gamers

Brainwaves are not merely a byproduct of brain activity; they are indicators of mental states. By observing brainwave patterns, gamers can identify when their brain is performing optimally and when it may be fatigued or unfocused. For example:

- Beta waves dominate when you are focused and engaged during high-speed, strategic games.

- Alpha waves emerge during post-game recovery and relaxation.
- Theta waves may highlight creative problem-solving or subconscious pattern recognition.

Learning to monitor, train, and optimize brainwave activity can help gamers improve focus, reaction time, and mental endurance—core components for peak performance.

Deep Dive into the Five Types of Brainwaves Frequencies

As mentioned earlier, your brain generates electrical activity that can be measured as brainwaves, categorized by their frequency. Each type corresponds to a particular mental state, ranging from deep relaxation to intense focus. Here's a breakdown of the five main types of brainwaves:

1. Delta Waves (0.5–4 Hz)
    a. State: Deep sleep and physical recovery.
    b. Why It Matters: While not directly related to gaming performance, delta waves are essential for rest and recovery. A well-rested brain will improve your focus and reaction time during gameplay.
2. Theta Waves (4–8 Hz)
    a. State: Light relaxation, meditation, and creativity.
    b. Why It Matters: Theta waves can help gamers tap into creativity, imagination, and a relaxed mindset—useful for strategic or exploratory games where creativity and calm thinking are needed.
3. Alpha Waves (8–12 Hz)
    a. State: Calm focus and readiness.
    b. Why It Matters: Alpha waves are crucial for maintaining a state of flow—a relaxed, alert state where you're highly focused but not stressed. This is often the "sweet spot" for

gamers who need sustained focus and mental clarity.
   4. Beta Waves (12–30 Hz)
      a. State: Active focus, alertness, and problem-solving.
      b. Why It Matters: Beta waves dominate when you're engaged in intense gameplay, solving problems, or making split-second decisions. However, too much beta activity can also lead to stress and mental fatigue, which is why balancing beta waves is key.
   5. Gamma Waves (30–50 Hz)
      a. State: High-level concentration, cognitive processing, and peak performance.
      b. Why It Matters: Gamma waves are linked to heightened focus and advanced cognitive processing—perfect for gamers aiming to process multiple inputs quickly, make critical decisions, and stay at their peak under pressure.

The Ideal Brainwave States for Gaming

Different games and tasks require different mental states. Here's how you can align your brainwave activity with the demands of your game:

- First-Person Shooters (FPS): A balance of beta and gamma waves for quick reflexes, sharp decision-making, and high focus.
- Strategy Games (RTS, MOBAs): More alpha and beta waves for calm concentration, multitasking, and tactical decision-making.
- Exploratory or Sandbox Games: Increased theta and alpha waves to encourage creativity, relaxation, and immersion.
- Competitive eSports: Sustaining alpha (calm focus) while engaging beta and gamma for peak performance under pressure.

Understanding this connection helps you tailor your brain training exercises and EEG routines to the specific demands of your preferred game genres.

Using EEG to Monitor Brainwaves
EEG devices like Emotiv Insight or Muse measure brainwave activity in real time, providing you with data on your mental states. With the right tools, you can monitor your brainwaves during gameplay to:

• Identify Patterns: Learn which brainwave states help you perform your best.
• Track Fatigue: Recognize when stress or mental exhaustion disrupts your focus.
• Train for Improvement: Practice exercises to enhance focus, reduce stress, and maintain flow.

Your brainwaves are the key to optimizing your gaming performance. By understanding how each brainwave works and using EEG devices to monitor your mental states, you can improve focus, reaction time, and overall performance. In the following sections, we'll explore how to train and balance these brainwaves to achieve your gaming goals.

1.3 Measuring and Interpreting your Brainwaves

Now that you understand the role of brainwaves in gaming, the next step is to measure and interpret your brainwave activity using EEG devices. This section will walk you through the tools, techniques, and methods for understanding what your brain is telling you and how you can use this knowledge to improve your gaming performance.

Choosing the Right EEG Device for Measurement
As we introduced earlier, EEG devices like Emotiv Insight and

Muse are popular, accessible tools for monitoring brainwave activity. Here's a brief overview of what each offers:

Emotiv Insight:
- Features: Multi-sensor device with real-time tracking of five brainwave types (delta, theta, alpha, beta, gamma).
- Strength: Offers detailed metrics and allows integration with various platforms for deeper analysis.
- Best For: Gamers looking for robust insights and advanced data.

Muse:
- Features: Lightweight and beginner-friendly with fewer sensors, focusing on meditation and calm focus.
- Strength: Simple to use, excellent for tracking relaxation and focus states.
- Best For: Gamers who are new to EEG and want a simple, effective tool to monitor focus.

Tip: Choose a device based on your goals—if you're aiming for peak performance and cognitive insights, go with a more advanced option like Emotiv. For basic tracking of calm and focus, Muse is an excellent starting point.

How EEG Devices Measure Brainwaves

EEG headsets work by detecting tiny electrical signals generated by neurons in your brain. These signals are measured in microvolts and categorized into brainwave types based on their frequency.

1. Sensors: Small electrodes in the headset detect electrical activity.
2. Signal Processing: The raw brainwave data is processed into readable formats on your device or app.
3. Visualization: Graphs, charts, and feedback dashboards help you interpret your brain activity in real time.

When using your EEG device, you'll typically see output data in the form of:

- Graphs: Show brainwave frequency (Hz) and amplitude over time.
- Focus Scores: Numerical representations of your mental state (e.g., focus level, calm level).
- Heat Maps: Visual summaries of brainwave intensity during specific activities.

Interpreting Brainwave Data

Understanding your EEG readings is key to improving performance. Here's how to interpret the main insights:

1. Calm vs. Active States:
   a. High Alpha/Theta: Indicates relaxation and calm focus—ideal for strategic or low-stress gaming.
   b. High Beta/Gamma: Reflects active concentration and decision-making—essential for fast-paced, competitive games.
2. Identifying Stress and Fatigue:
   a. Excessive Beta Waves: May indicate stress, overthinking, or mental fatigue.
   b. Low Alpha Levels: Suggest difficulty maintaining calm focus under pressure.
   c. Solution: Use relaxation techniques to balance your brainwave activity (covered in upcoming sections).
3. Finding Your Flow State:
   a. A "flow state" combines alpha and beta activity. Your EEG data will show balanced waves when you're fully immersed and performing at your peak.
   b. Use your readings to identify when you enter this state naturally and learn how to replicate it consistently.

Tracking Patterns Over Time
To get the most out of your EEG data:

- Measure Regularly: Monitor your brainwaves during different gaming sessions—practice, tournaments, and casual play.
- Analyze Trends: Look for patterns in your focus, stress, and relaxation levels. Are there times of day or types of games where you perform better?
- Adjust Accordingly: Use the insights to modify your routines and mental training exercises to sustain optimal performance.

Practical Example
Let's say you measure your brainwaves during a competitive first-person shooter game. Your EEG readings show:

- High Beta Waves: Intense focus and decision-making.
- Spike in Beta after a loss: Indicates stress and frustration.

With this data, you can:

1. Take short breaks during intense gaming sessions to reset your mental state.
2. Practice breathing exercises to balance beta waves and prevent burnout.
3. Train to sustain alpha waves during high-pressure moments for calm focus.

Measuring and interpreting your brainwaves is the foundation of brainwave training for gamers. By selecting the right EEG device, understanding your brainwave data, and identifying patterns over time, you'll be equipped with the insights needed to improve focus, manage stress, and find your flow state. In the next section, we'll explore tools and exercises you can use to train your brainwaves for better gaming performance.

1.4 Practical Exercises to Improve Focus and

Reaction Time

Now that you understand how to measure and interpret your brainwaves, it's time to put that knowledge into action. This section introduces targeted exercises designed to improve your focus, reaction time, and overall gaming performance using EEG devices. These exercises will help you train your brain to enter optimal states for peak performance.

1. Focus Training with Real-Time EEG Feedback

EEG devices like Emotiv Insight and Muse offer real-time feedback on your focus levels. Here's a simple exercise:

- Setup: Wear your EEG headset and launch the app's focus-tracking tool.
- Task: Start with a basic, distraction-free activity like watching a dot on a screen, reading a page of text, or listening to calm music. Monitor your focus scores on the app. The goal is to increase your focus levels over time.
- Challenge: Gradually introduce distractions (e.g., background noise, timers) to train your brain to stay focused under pressure, similar to gaming environments.

Pro Tip: Set a timer for 10 minutes daily. Consistent practice helps you build mental endurance, which translates directly to longer periods of sharp focus during gaming.

2. Reaction Time Enhancement with Visual and Audio Cues

Reaction time is critical for competitive gaming, especially in fast-paced genres like FPS or MOBAs. Here's how to train it:

- Setup: Use an EEG headset to monitor your brainwave activity while performing reaction drills.
- Exercise: Download a reaction training app or use a simple online tool like a Reaction Time Tester (look for apps with visual or audio cues). Focus on the cue—whether a flash of light, a beep, or an on-screen prompt—and respond as quickly as possible. Check your EEG data to identify patterns: Are beta or gamma waves spiking? How does stress

(excessive beta) impact your reaction speed?
- Progression: As you improve, increase the difficulty of the reaction drills by adding multitasking elements or reducing cue visibility.

Pro Tip: Combine reaction drills with mindfulness breathing techniques (covered next) to help balance focus and reduce mental stress during gameplay.

3. Breathing Exercises for Calm Focus

Breathing exercises help regulate brainwave activity, reduce stress, and improve focus—essential for staying sharp during long gaming sessions.

- Setup: Wear your EEG headset and monitor your alpha and beta waves.
- Exercise: Inhale deeply through your nose for 4 seconds. Hold your breath for 4 seconds. Exhale slowly through your mouth for 6 seconds. Repeat this cycle for 2-3 minutes.
- Goal: Watch your EEG data. Alpha waves (relaxed focus) should increase, and beta waves (stress) should stabilize.

Pro Tip: Perform this exercise before gaming sessions or during breaks to reset your brain and regain focus.

4. Multi-Tasking Focus Drill

In many games, multi-tasking is key to winning—monitoring the map, tracking opponents, and executing actions simultaneously. Here's how to train your brain for multitasking:

- Setup: Use your EEG device and a multi-tasking app or game (like a simple puzzle game combined with a secondary task, e.g., listening to audio instructions).
- Exercise: Monitor your EEG readings while juggling two tasks. Identify when your focus dips (beta waves drop, or alpha waves spike), and push yourself to maintain focus on both tasks.
- Progression: Gradually increase the complexity of the tasks as

your ability to focus under pressure improves.

5. Visualization and Mental Rehearsal

Visualization is a powerful tool for improving performance and focus. Athletes and professional gamers use it to mentally rehearse high-pressure situations.

- Setup: Find a quiet space, wear your EEG headset, and sit comfortably.
- Exercise: Close your eyes and visualize yourself playing your game of choice flawlessly. Picture yourself making quick decisions, executing perfect strategies, and achieving victory. Track your EEG readings—alpha waves should dominate, indicating a relaxed but focused state.
- Goal: Practice visualization daily for 5-10 minutes to build confidence, reduce anxiety, and improve mental preparedness.

Pro Tip: Combine visualization exercises with deep breathing for maximum benefit.

By incorporating these exercises into your routine, you'll notice significant improvements in focus, reaction time, and your ability to stay calm under pressure. EEG tools allow you to measure progress objectively, ensuring that your brain training efforts translate directly to better gaming performance.

1.5 Step-by-Step Tutorial: Improving Focus Using EEG

This exercise will help you enhance focus and track changes in brain activity using your EEG device.

Step 1: Set Up Your EEG Device

Power on your EEG headset (e.g., Emotiv Insight or Muse). Connect it to your computer or mobile app following the device instructions. Ensure the headset is comfortably placed and all electrodes are making proper contact with your scalp. Confirm the app shows stable readings for brainwaves (like Alpha, Beta, etc.).

Step 2: Establish Your Baseline Brainwaves
Sit in a quiet, distraction-free environment. Close your eyes and relax for two minutes while the EEG headset records your baseline brain activity. Take note of your Alpha waves (related to calmness) and Beta waves (related to focus) in your app's brainwave display.

Step 3: Perform a Focus Task
Choose a simple focus exercise, such as staring at a single object (e.g., a pen or a dot on paper) for 2–3 minutes or reading a short passage while eliminating distractions. As you focus, observe the EEG app. Look for an increase in Beta wave activity, indicating improved attention.

Step 4: Reflect on Your Results
Compare the brainwave data from your baseline and focus task. Note if Beta waves increased during the activity. If your focus was disrupted, identify what broke your attention and repeat the task.

Step-by-Step Tutorial: Reaction Time Training with EEG
This exercise will help you sharpen your reaction time using EEG feedback.

Step 1: Prepare Your EEG Setup
Follow the same device setup process as in the previous tutorial. Open the EEG app or software that shows real-time brainwave changes.

Step 2: Choose a Reaction Time Activity
Select activities like light-based exercises, using apps or online games that flash colors requiring quick clicks or taps, or sound-based exercises, where you respond quickly to audible cues (like a beep or tone).

Step 3: Track Your Brainwaves During the Task

Monitor Beta waves for focus and Theta waves for distraction. Complete 3–5 rounds of the chosen activity while staying fully engaged.

Step 4: Analyze Your Results
Review your EEG data to see patterns. For example, were Beta waves steady during the reaction time exercises? Did Theta waves spike during moments of distraction? Repeat the exercise daily and aim to maintain steady Beta waves for longer durations.

1.6 Focus Techniques for Competitive Gaming

In competitive gaming, maintaining laser-sharp focus can mean the difference between victory and defeat. Whether you're navigating fast-paced FPS battles, strategizing in MOBAs, or playing high-intensity racing games, focus is a critical mental skill that separates top-tier players from the rest. EEG tools provide an excellent way to monitor and improve focus, but you'll also need practical techniques to complement your brainwave training.

1. Single-Task Focus
Many gamers lose focus because they try to multitask – glancing at messages, listening to podcasts, or toggling between screens. Top players emphasize single-task focus to stay in the zone.

Practice Tip: Dedicate short 20–30-minute sessions to uninterrupted gameplay. Use EEG feedback to monitor your brainwaves and identify when your focus drifts. Over time, train yourself to extend these periods of deep focus.

2. Reducing Distractions
External distractions like background noise, notifications, or cluttered setups can pull you out of your peak performance state.

Actionable Steps:
- Create a dedicated gaming space that's quiet and free of distractions.
- Use noise-canceling headphones or white noise to block out

external sounds.
- Turn off notifications on your devices during gaming sessions.

3. Focused Attention Bursts
Your brain is not wired to sustain intense focus indefinitely. Professional gamers often use short bursts of high focus followed by quick breaks to recharge.

Technique: Play for 25 minutes with full concentration, then take a 5-minute break. Use your EEG device to monitor how focus levels change during these bursts. Track patterns over time to see what works best for you.

4. Visualization for Enhanced Focus
Visualization techniques help prime your mind for success and improve your focus under pressure. Before starting a session, take a moment to mentally "walk through" the gameplay. Picture the moves you'll make, anticipate challenges, and see yourself executing each step successfully.

Practice Tip: Use your EEG headset to monitor relaxation and focus levels during visualization. Combine deep breathing with this exercise to get into an optimal mental state.

5. Short Meditative Resets
A quick mental reset can work wonders if you feel your focus slipping mid-game. Meditative techniques like box breathing or quick mindfulness exercises can bring you back into the zone.

Example Exercise: Inhale for 4 seconds, hold for 4 seconds, exhale for 4 seconds, hold again for 4 seconds. Repeat this cycle for 2–3 minutes to reset your focus. Use EEG to observe how your brainwaves shift into a calmer, more focused state.

By combining these focus techniques with EEG feedback, you can optimize your brain's ability to sustain focus during gameplay. Start small – integrate one or two methods into your routine and monitor the impact. Over time, you'll gain the mental edge needed to perform at your best, game after game.

1.7 Relaxation Strategies for Better Performance

While focus is critical in gaming, staying relaxed is equally important to avoid burnout, tension, and decision fatigue. Excessive stress and overstimulation can disrupt your reaction time, cause impulsive decisions, and lower overall performance. EEG devices allow you to measure brainwave activity, specifically alpha waves, which are associated with relaxation and calm states. Here are some strategies to incorporate relaxation into your gaming routine:

1. Pre-Game Breathing Exercises
Calming your mind before a gaming session helps you start in an optimal mental state.

Box Breathing Technique: Inhale for 4 seconds, hold for 4 seconds, exhale for 4 seconds, and hold for another 4 seconds. Repeat for 3–5 minutes.

EEG Tip: Use your headset to track the shift in your brainwaves as you transition into a relaxed state, ensuring you're primed for focus.

2. Short Mindful Breaks
During intense gaming sessions, it's easy to lose track of your body and mind. Incorporating mindful breaks helps reset your mental state, relax tense muscles, and improve clarity.

Steps for a 2-Minute Reset:
1. Pause your game and sit comfortably.
2. Close your eyes and take slow, deep breaths, focusing on your inhale and exhale.
3. Use EEG to observe brainwave shifts, noting when you re-enter a calm state.

3. Progressive Muscle Relaxation (PMR)

PMR is an excellent tool for relieving physical tension that accumulates during long hours of gaming.

How to Practice: Start from your feet and work upward. Tense each muscle group for 5–10 seconds, then release and feel the relaxation spread through your body. Combine this with EEG to monitor when you reach a fully relaxed state.

4. Visualization for Calm Performance
Similar to focus visualization, you can use imagery to calm your nerves and reduce stress before a competitive game.

How to Do It: Picture a calm scene – like a serene beach or a quiet forest. As you visualize, focus on slow breathing and use EEG to track an increase in alpha waves, which signify relaxation.

5. Post-Game Cool Down
Ending a gaming session with relaxation techniques helps your brain and body recover. It's particularly useful after high-stress, high-stakes games.

Practical Example: Spend 5–10 minutes listening to calming music, practicing gentle breathing, or stretching. Use your EEG headset to monitor your brain's transition into a restful state.

Why It Works
The ability to switch between intense focus and relaxation is a hallmark of top performers across disciplines, from esports players to elite athletes. By actively practicing relaxation strategies and monitoring EEG feedback, you train your brain to recover faster and handle stressful situations with ease. This balance ultimately improves endurance, reaction times, and your ability to make smart decisions under pressure.

1.8 Combining EEG with Mindfulness for Peak Performance

Mindfulness is a mental practice focused on staying present and aware in the moment without judgment. For gamers, mindfulness enhances clarity, reduces distractions, and improves decision-making under pressure. EEG devices allow you to see how mindfulness influences your brainwaves in real time, providing tangible feedback for refining your practice.

Why Mindfulness Matters in Gaming

Gaming demands rapid responses and heightened focus, but it can also create mental clutter, frustration, and overstimulation. Mindfulness trains your brain to stay calm and steady during high-intensity sessions. Combining mindfulness with EEG lets you:

- Identify when you're overly tense (high beta waves).
- Encourage calm focus (alpha waves).
- Build awareness of your mental patterns during gaming sessions.

Mindful Breathing with EEG

This technique uses your breath to calm the mind and center your focus.

Steps to Practice:

1. Put on your EEG headset. Start by sitting comfortably and focusing on slow, rhythmic breathing.
2. Inhale deeply for 4–5 seconds, hold for 2–3 seconds, and exhale slowly.
3. Observe your EEG feedback. As you breathe, watch for a rise in alpha waves (relaxation) and a reduction in beta waves (stress).

Tip: Use this exercise before and during breaks in a gaming session to reset and improve focus.

Body Scan Meditation for Relaxation

The body scan helps gamers identify physical and mental tension, releasing stress in the process.

How to Practice:

1. Begin at your feet and slowly shift attention up through

your body, noticing areas of tightness.
2. Pair this practice with EEG to monitor your brainwaves. You'll likely see a decrease in beta activity as you relax deeper into the exercise.
3. Regular practice makes you more aware of early signs of tension during gaming, allowing you to adjust.

Single-Task Focus Exercise
Mindfulness emphasizes single-task attention, which directly translates to improved in-game focus and decision-making.

Practice:
1. Set your EEG device to track focus levels (beta waves).
2. Perform a simple task – like tracking a moving object on the screen – for 5 minutes.
3. When your mind wanders, gently redirect attention and note how the EEG data shifts as your focus improves.

Over time, this exercise strengthens your ability to stay in the zone during complex gameplay.

Mindful Cool Down After Gaming
After a gaming session, mindfulness helps you transition from high-intensity focus to a relaxed state. This reduces mental fatigue and improves your ability to recover for future sessions.

Practical Steps:
1. Sit in a quiet space and practice mindful breathing for 5–10 minutes.
2. Monitor EEG changes, noting how your brainwaves shift from high beta (focus) to alpha (relaxation).
3. Use this data to refine your post-game recovery routine.

The Science Behind It
Mindfulness practices have been shown to improve brain plasticity, or the brain's ability to adapt and strengthen connections. By using EEG to observe your progress, you gain measurable insights into your mental growth and performance

improvement.

1.9 Managing Gaming Fatigue with EEG Insights

Long gaming sessions can lead to mental fatigue, reduced reaction times, and a decline in focus. EEG devices offer real-time data to help you identify signs of mental exhaustion and create personalized strategies for recovery. By learning to recognize when your brain needs a break, you can prevent burnout and perform better over time.

Why Gaming Fatigue Happens
Fatigue sets in when your brain becomes overstimulated or overworked, especially during high-intensity gaming sessions. This often leads to:

- A drop in focus (beta wave decline).
- Overactivity in stress-related brainwaves.
- Poor decision-making and slower reaction times.

Monitoring your brainwaves with EEG allows you to spot early indicators of fatigue before they start impacting your gameplay.

Key EEG Signals for Fatigue
1. Beta Wave Drop-Off: Beta waves are associated with active focus and alertness. A sudden decline suggests reduced mental energy.
2. Rising Theta Waves: Theta waves often increase when you're zoning out or daydreaming – a clear sign your mind is wandering.
3. Stress Indicators: Persistent high beta waves, paired with low alpha activity, may signal mental strain and overstimulation.

By identifying these patterns, you can schedule breaks and recovery strategies tailored to your needs.

Practical Strategies for Managing Fatigue

1. Short, Regular Breaks (5-10 Minutes)
    a. Set a timer to take a break every 45–60 minutes of gameplay. Use EEG to observe how quickly your brain returns to relaxed alpha states during breaks.
    b. Activities like slow breathing, light stretching, or listening to calm music can accelerate recovery.
2. The Power of Micro-Rests
    a. In the middle of a gaming session, take 1–2 minutes to close your eyes and focus on deep breathing.
    b. Monitor EEG signals to track reductions in stress-related beta activity. Over time, this habit can prevent cumulative fatigue.
3. Sleep and Brainwave Recovery
    a. Quality sleep is critical for peak mental performance. Use EEG data to monitor brainwave activity before bed. If you see persistent high beta waves, it's a sign to unwind with relaxation exercises.
    b. Sleep helps restore healthy theta and delta wave activity, improving focus and energy the next day.
4. Recovery Journaling with EEG Data
    a. Use a journal to log fatigue patterns observed in your EEG data. Note when focus starts to drop, what triggers fatigue, and which recovery techniques work best for you.
    b. Over time, you'll identify trends that help you create an optimal gaming schedule.

The Long-Term Benefits
Gamers who proactively manage fatigue perform better, maintain sharper focus, and reduce the risk of burnout. Using EEG to fine-tune your routine ensures you're consistently gaming at your best

without sacrificing your mental well-being.

1.10 Using EEG Data to Analyze and Improve Performance

In this section, we'll explore how to leverage EEG data to identify your strengths, weaknesses, and opportunities for improvement as a gamer. EEG data can provide valuable insights into your mental states during gameplay, helping you fine-tune your strategies and train more effectively.

1. Understanding EEG Metrics for Performance Analysis

To analyze and improve performance, it's essential to understand the key EEG metrics:

- Focus Levels: Measured primarily through beta waves, focus metrics help you identify periods of peak concentration and areas where your focus drops.
- Relaxation States: Dominated by alpha waves, relaxation states indicate when you're too calm or unfocused.
- Mental Fatigue: Sustained beta wave activity with little fluctuation can suggest fatigue, which impacts reaction time and decision-making.
- Stress Responses: Spikes in high-beta or gamma waves during critical moments can highlight pressure points or stress triggers during gameplay.

Pro Tip: Compare EEG data from different gaming sessions to pinpoint consistent patterns. For example, do focus levels drop during long matches or under specific in-game scenarios?

2. Recording and Reviewing EEG Data

Start by tracking EEG data during your gaming sessions. Follow these steps to gather and interpret data effectively:

- Setup: Use an EEG headset like Emotiv or Muse and pair it with EEG software that can log data over time.
- Gameplay Session: Record EEG data while playing for 20-30

minutes. Focus on specific goals—monitoring focus, stress, or fatigue at critical moments.
- Post-Session Review: Analyze the data to identify trends. For instance:
    - When did focus peak or drop?
    - Were there moments of high stress?
    - Did fatigue set in during longer sessions?

Actionable Insight: Highlight key sections of gameplay (e.g., intense battles, boss fights) where focus or stress readings stood out. Use these insights to tweak your gameplay strategy or take breaks to avoid mental fatigue.

3. Identifying Your Focus Zones

EEG data can help you determine your focus zones—periods where your attention and reaction times are at their best. Here's how to identify them:

- Analyze Consistency: Do you perform better in the first 10 minutes of gameplay, or do you hit your stride later?
- Break Down Performance: Use EEG data to assess individual components of a game (e.g., aiming, decision-making, map awareness). Identify where you excel and where focus falters.
- Visualize Patterns: Many EEG apps offer graphical data (e.g., focus or relaxation curves). Use these visuals to spot trends and adjust your routine accordingly.

4. Addressing Weaknesses and Building Strengths

Use EEG insights to target areas for improvement and reinforce your strengths:

- Reducing Stress: If EEG data shows stress spikes during critical moments, practice breathing exercises or mindfulness drills (covered earlier) to remain calm under pressure.
- Boosting Reaction Time: If your focus levels drop during fast-paced action, integrate reaction training drills into your routine. Monitor improvements with EEG feedback.

- Improving Endurance: If fatigue becomes a recurring issue, use EEG data to schedule breaks and adjust gameplay sessions for better stamina.

Pro Tip: Combine EEG analysis with performance metrics from your game (e.g., accuracy, reaction speed, win rates). This holistic approach gives you a clearer picture of your mental and physical performance.

5. Creating a Feedback Loop for Continuous Improvement
The real power of EEG lies in its ability to help you monitor progress over time. Here's how to create a simple feedback loop:

1. Track: Record EEG data during each session and identify trends (e.g., focus zones, stress spikes).
2. Reflect: Analyze the data and correlate it with gameplay outcomes. What patterns emerge?
3. Adjust: Implement changes to your strategy or training routine based on the insights (e.g., adding focus drills, improving stress management).
4. Repeat: Continuously monitor EEG data to measure improvements and refine your approach.

Actionable Example: After a week of tracking, you notice that focus dips occur consistently during the mid-game phase. To counter this, you integrate short mindfulness exercises during breaks and monitor how focus levels improve.

By using EEG data as a tool for reflection and improvement, you can train smarter, play more efficiently, and achieve measurable gains in your performance. Whether you're aiming for better focus, faster reactions, or stress control, EEG provides a scientific and objective way to elevate your game.

1.11 Case Studies: Gamers Who Enhanced their Performance

In this section, we explore real-world examples and hypothetical scenarios showcasing how EEG technology has been used to improve focus, reaction times, and overall gaming performance. By sharing these experiences, readers can gain practical insights into what's possible and find inspiration for their own EEG-enhanced journeys.

1. Competitive Gamer Boosts Reaction Time with EEG Training

Meet Alex, a competitive esports player specializing in fast-paced shooter games. Struggling with reaction delays during tournaments, Alex incorporated EEG headsets into their daily training routine. Using tools like Emotiv Insights, Alex tracked their brainwave activity during intense gaming sessions. Over several weeks, EEG data revealed periods of distraction and mental fatigue.

Through focused breathing exercises and mindfulness training based on EEG feedback, Alex improved their beta brainwave activity, leading to faster reaction times and more consistent in-game performance. By the end of the experiment, Alex reported a 15% improvement in reaction times and a noticeable confidence boost during competitions.

2. Amateur Player Achieves Better Focus in Strategy Games

Samantha, an avid fan of real-time strategy (RTS) games, often struggled to stay focused during lengthy matches. Samantha started using a Muse EEG headset to measure her brainwaves while gaming. By analyzing her alpha and beta brainwave patterns, Samantha pinpointed moments when her focus dipped due to external distractions or mental overload.

She implemented EEG-guided focus drills, like short meditation sessions before matches and quick breaks when her brainwave data indicated signs of mental fatigue. Within weeks, Samantha noticed greater clarity in decision-making and was able to sustain deep focus for longer stretches. This resulted in more strategic victories and a newfound enjoyment of the game.

3. Using EEG to Recover from Mental Burnout

Jake, a competitive gamer, faced mental burnout after months of non-stop tournaments. He turned to EEG-based techniques to identify his stress triggers and optimize recovery. By monitoring theta brainwave activity during rest periods, Jake learned to incorporate guided relaxation exercises to re-center his mental state.

Over time, EEG tracking helped Jake balance his training load, prioritize mental recovery, and rebuild his focus without pushing himself to exhaustion. He shared that EEG-guided relaxation became an essential part of his recovery process, improving his overall well-being and performance.

4. Hypothetical Scenario: Team Training with EEG for Optimal Performance

Imagine a competitive esports team preparing for a major tournament. Each team member uses EEG devices to identify their unique cognitive strengths and weaknesses. The coach leverages the EEG data to optimize practice sessions, ensuring players focus on improving attention, reducing stress, and enhancing reaction times. For example, one player might focus on deep-focus exercises, while another might practice EEG-assisted relaxation techniques.

The team collectively achieves greater mental resilience, synchronization, and focus during high-stress matches, leading to improved coordination and success.

1.12 Building a Routine for Peak Gaming Performance

In this section, we bring together everything covered in the book to help readers design a practical and sustainable routine for improving their gaming performance using EEG. Building consistency is the key to long-term success, and this section offers a step-by-step guide to creating an EEG-based training plan.

The first step is identifying your gaming goals. Start by reflecting on what you want to achieve. Are you looking to improve focus, reaction time, stress management, or overall mental endurance during long gaming sessions? Defining clear and specific goals will help you tailor your EEG-based routine to your needs. Example goals include improving focus for competitive tournaments, reducing mental fatigue during marathons, training faster reaction times, or managing stress during high-pressure games. Write down your goals and revisit them weekly to track your progress.

Once you've clarified your goals, it's time to design your EEG training routine. A sample framework might look like this:

In the morning, spend 15-20 minutes on mindfulness or breathing exercises while monitoring alpha brainwaves using EEG. This prepares your mind for a productive gaming session. Optionally, run a focus calibration session with your EEG headset to gauge your mental baseline for the day.

Before gameplay, allocate 5-10 minutes to warm up with EEG monitoring. Practice a short focus exercise, like visualization or light meditation, to boost beta brainwaves and sharpen attention.

During gameplay, use EEG tools to monitor your real-time brainwave activity. Take note of when focus dips or stress rises, and schedule micro-breaks when EEG data signals fatigue. For example, rest for 2-3 minutes after every hour of intense play to recharge.

After gaming, dedicate 10-15 minutes to a post-game recovery routine. Use EEG-guided relaxation exercises or breathing techniques to bring down stress and promote recovery. Monitor your brainwaves to ensure your brain shifts into a restful state, such as generating more alpha or theta waves.

Consistency is essential, so aim to follow this routine daily or at least three to five times per week. Keeping a journal to record EEG data alongside subjective feedback—like energy levels, focus, and stress—can help you tweak and optimize your routine. Over time, this habit will lead to noticeable improvements in your mental performance and overall gaming experience.

By building a structured and EEG-informed routine, you empower yourself to achieve peak gaming performance while also promoting healthier mental habits. This routine can be customized to fit your schedule, needs, and EEG insights, making it a flexible and sustainable part of your life.

1.13 Building Long-Term Gaming Habits with EEG

Improving your gaming skills isn't just about short-term gains – it's about building sustainable habits that ensure long-term success. EEG data can help you identify patterns, reinforce good habits, and create consistent routines that optimize your focus, energy, and control over time.

Why Building Habits Matters
Habits form the foundation for improvement in any area, including gaming. By training your brain to consistently achieve focused, relaxed, and high-performance states, you can:

- Improve reaction times and decision-making.
- Develop better stress management during competitive play.
- Increase your stamina and avoid burnout.

Using EEG as a tool to track and refine your brain's responses helps you build habits based on real data rather than guesswork.

Steps to Create Long-Term Gaming Habits
1. Start with Clear Goals
    a. Use EEG to monitor your baseline brainwave activity during gaming. Set small, measurable goals, such as increasing time spent in a focused state (beta waves) or reducing stress (high beta spikes).
    b. Example: "I want to maintain high beta activity

for 20 minutes without drops."
2. Track Progress and Reflect
   a. Use an EEG journal to record daily sessions, noting focus improvements, reaction times, and mental energy.
   b. Include specific EEG observations: "My focus dropped at minute 25, suggesting I need a short break earlier."
3. Use Feedback Loops for Continuous Improvement
   a. EEG offers immediate feedback on how your brain reacts to different strategies. If you see an increase in focus after a particular exercise, integrate it into your routine.
   b. Example: Monitor alpha wave increases after a short meditation session and adjust your warm-up routine accordingly.
4. Reinforce Good Habits with Rewards
   a. Positive reinforcement strengthens new habits. After reaching EEG-based milestones (e.g., improved beta wave consistency), reward yourself with something enjoyable – a break, music, or a small treat.
5. Consistency is Key
   a. Building habits takes time. Incorporate EEG tracking into your routine at least 3–4 times a week to monitor your progress and fine-tune your techniques.
   b. Use small, consistent changes rather than overwhelming yourself with too many goals at once.

Examples of Habit-Building with EEG
- Focus Training: Start each gaming session with 5 minutes of EEG-monitored focus exercises. Over time, this routine trains your brain to enter a focused state faster.
- Fatigue Management: Schedule breaks based on EEG fatigue

signals to develop a rhythm that sustains your performance.
- Stress Reduction: Integrate relaxation techniques when high beta activity spikes, helping you stay calm under pressure.

The Power of Long-Term Growth

By tracking EEG data, reinforcing habits, and continually improving, you can create a cycle of growth that maximizes your gaming performance. Whether you're playing for fun or competing at the highest level, these sustainable habits will ensure you perform at your peak for years to come.

CHAPTER 2: EXPLORING BCI GAMING – PLAYING GAMES WITH YOUR BRAIN

Gaming has always been about pushing boundaries—immersive graphics, complex narratives, and fast-paced action have taken us to new heights. But what if you could play games using nothing but your brainwaves? Brain-Computer Interface (BCI) gaming represents the cutting edge of innovation in the gaming world, enabling players to interact with games using their thoughts and mental focus. It's not just science fiction anymore; BCI gaming is here, and it's transforming the way we think about gameplay and engagement.

In this chapter, we'll dive into the exciting world of BCI gaming. You'll discover how these systems work, what it takes to get started, and how brainwave technology is being integrated into games. Whether you're curious about beginner-friendly games or dreaming of mastering advanced BCI control, this chapter will give you the tools and knowledge to unlock new levels of interactive play. Get ready to play with your brain and discover a whole new frontier in gaming.

2.1 Introduction to Brain-Computer Interface Game

BCI gaming represents one of the most exciting frontiers in modern technology. Unlike traditional gaming, which relies on controllers, keyboards, or touchscreens, BCI games allow you to interact and control gameplay directly with your mind. By leveraging EEG (electroencephalogram) technology, these systems interpret brainwave activity and translate it into commands within the game environment. This fascinating blend of neuroscience and gaming technology not only redefines how games are played but also offers a glimpse into the future of immersive, hands-free experiences.

What Makes BCI Gaming Unique?
At its core, BCI gaming removes the physical barrier between you and the game. Instead of pressing buttons, your brainwaves act as the input. Think of it this way: when you focus, relax, or imagine a specific movement, your brain generates electrical signals. EEG headsets detect these signals and send them to the game, allowing you to control in-game actions such as moving a character, selecting an object, or even performing a task—just by thinking.

For example, focusing intensely on a specific object might propel a character forward, while relaxing could slow down the gameplay. It's both intuitive and challenging because the controls are not about dexterity but about mastering your mental states.

A Glimpse Into the Technology
BCI gaming relies on EEG headsets—wearable devices that detect and record brainwave activity. While early BCI systems were confined to research labs, recent advancements have made them commercially available and affordable for everyday users. Devices like Emotiv Insight and Muse have paved the way for practical,

accessible BCI gaming, enabling anyone with curiosity and a headset to start exploring.

Who Is BCI Gaming For?
BCI gaming attracts a wide range of audiences:

- Gamers: Those who love experimenting with cutting-edge technology and want to challenge themselves in new ways.
- Tech Enthusiasts: People excited about innovation and the intersection of mind and machine.
- Researchers: Those studying cognitive performance, brainwaves, or human-computer interaction.
- Accessibility Advocates: BCI gaming has the potential to make gaming more inclusive for individuals with physical limitations, as it bypasses the need for traditional controllers.

The Future is Now
While still emerging, BCI gaming is already making significant strides in the gaming industry. From simple brainwave-based games that test focus and relaxation to advanced platforms exploring brain control in virtual reality, BCI represents a major leap forward. For gamers and developers alike, this technology is not just a concept—it's a reality that's transforming the way we think about gaming.

In the following sections, we'll explore the technology behind BCI, show you how to set up your own EEG gaming environment, and introduce practical exercises to help you master brainwave control for an exciting, immersive experience.

2.2 Getting Started with BCI Devices

Stepping into the world of BCI gaming may seem complex at first, but it's surprisingly accessible thanks to advancements in EEG technology. In this section, we'll break down everything you need to know to get started with BCI devices, including choosing the right equipment, setting it up, and preparing your mind for success.

Choosing the Right BCI Device

The first step in getting started is selecting the appropriate EEG headset. While there are many options on the market, two popular choices stand out for their accessibility, affordability, and user-friendliness:

1. Emotiv Insight:
    a. Overview: A sleek, five-channel EEG headset designed for general brainwave tracking and BCI applications.
    b. Pros: Highly accurate, lightweight, and user-friendly. It integrates well with apps and games designed for brainwave control.
    c. Cons: Slightly more expensive than some alternatives, but ideal for both beginners and advanced users.
2. Muse:
    a. Overview: Primarily marketed for meditation and mindfulness, the Muse headset can also be adapted for simple BCI gaming.
    b. Pros: Affordable, easy to use, and great for exercises that focus on relaxation and mental states.
    c. Cons: Limited number of channels, making it less precise for complex BCI applications.

Which to Choose?

If you want precision, more channels, and broader BCI capabilities: Emotiv Insight. But if you're just starting and want an affordable, beginner-friendly option: Muse.

Setting Up Your BCI Device

Once you've chosen your headset, follow these simple steps to set it up:

1. Charge Your Device: Ensure the headset is fully charged

or connected to a power source.
2. Position the Headset Correctly: Follow the manufacturer's instructions to place the device securely on your head. Most devices require electrodes to make contact with specific areas of the scalp.
3. Connect to Your Computer or Smartphone: Download the necessary apps or software (e.g., Emotiv PRO, Muse app) and pair your device via Bluetooth.
4. Calibrate Your Brainwaves: Many EEG devices require an initial calibration step. This process involves performing specific mental tasks (like relaxing or focusing) to allow the device to recognize your brainwave patterns.

Preparing for Your First BCI Experience

BCI gaming relies on mental clarity, focus, and patience. Here are a few tips to prepare:

- Create a Quiet Environment: Minimize distractions like noise, bright lights, or interruptions.
- Relax Your Mind: Start with a few minutes of deep breathing or meditation to calm your brain activity.
- Set Realistic Expectations: BCI gaming requires practice. The first few sessions will involve learning how to generate the right brainwave states to control the game.
- Stay Consistent: As with any skill, consistency is key. Regular practice will improve your ability to interact with BCI games.

Exploring Compatible Games and Software

Many platforms and apps now offer BCI-compatible games and tools, such as:

- Mind Games: Focus-based games that require you to concentrate to move objects or achieve tasks.
- Meditation Apps: Games that respond to your ability to relax and reduce stress levels.
- Custom Software: Advanced users can explore platforms like Emotiv's developer tools to create their own BCI experiences.

DEEP DIVE: Popular EEG and BCI Devices for Gaming

To help you choose the right EEG or BCI device for your gaming journey, we're providing an in-depth comparison of popular tools available today. These devices range from affordable, user-friendly options to advanced systems for serious enthusiasts.

1. Emotiv Insight

Key Features: Wireless, lightweight, and portable EEG headset designed for focus and emotional monitoring.

Use Case: Ideal for gamers looking to monitor focus and stress while improving cognitive skills during gameplay.

Pros:
- Easy to set up with intuitive software.
- Affordable compared to high-end BCI systems.
- Great for tracking focus, relaxation, and mental states.

Cons:
- Lower signal resolution than research-grade devices.
- Limited direct integration with advanced BCI games.

Price (as of 2024): Approximately $300.

2. Muse S

Key Features: EEG headset tailored for brainwave-guided meditation and relaxation, with options to measure focus.

Use Case: Gamers can use Muse S to improve focus and calmness during intense game sessions. Excellent for stress relief and pre-game preparation.

Pros:
- Comfortable and designed for long sessions.
- Strong features for mindfulness and focus-building routines.
- Simple mobile app integration.

Cons:
- Primarily designed for meditation rather than active BCI

gaming.
- Slightly more expensive than basic EEG devices.

Price (as of 2024): Approximately $350.

3. OpenBCI Headsets

Key Features: Open-source EEG and BCI devices designed for advanced enthusiasts, researchers, and developers.

Use Case: Perfect for gamers or developers who want to customize their BCI experiences and create brain-controlled games.

Pros:
- High signal resolution for serious brainwave tracking.
- Fully customizable software for advanced users.
- Allows direct integration with BCI games.

Cons:
- Requires technical expertise for setup and use.
- Higher cost compared to commercial devices.

Price (as of 2024): Starts at $500–$1,000, depending on configuration.

4. NeuroSky MindWave

Key Features: Entry-level EEG headset designed for focus and brainwave monitoring with simple applications.

Use Case: A great starter device for gamers interested in experimenting with focus tracking on a budget.

Pros:
- Very affordable and beginner-friendly.
- Basic software for monitoring brainwaves.

Cons:
- Limited functionality compared to more advanced devices.
- May not support long-term focus training goals.

Price (as of 2024): Approximately $150–$200.

Choosing the Right Device

When selecting an EEG or BCI device for gaming, consider the following:

- Budget: Are you looking for a cost-effective option, or are you ready to invest in advanced tools?
- Purpose: Do you want to improve focus, reduce stress, or engage in brain-controlled games?
- Ease of Use: Beginners might prefer Emotiv Insight or Muse S, while tech enthusiasts could explore OpenBCI.
- Compatibility: Ensure the device supports the software or games you're most interested in using.

By understanding these devices and their strengths, you'll be able to make an informed choice that aligns with your personal goals, budget, and skill level.

2.3 How BCI-Controlled Games Work

BCI games are unique because they allow players to interact with virtual environments using their brain activity instead of traditional controllers. This section explores the mechanics behind BCI games, how brainwaves control actions, and the fascinating role of EEG devices in making this experience possible.

The Basics of BCI Gaming

At the heart of BCI games lies the principle of detecting and interpreting brain activity. EEG devices measure electrical signals produced by the brain, known as brainwaves, and translate these signals into commands that interact with the game.

Here's how the process works step by step:

1. Brainwave Detection: The EEG headset collects real-time brainwave data from your scalp. Different mental states (e.g., focus, relaxation, excitement) generate distinct brainwave patterns.
2. Signal Processing: The brainwave signals are processed by software to identify patterns that correspond to specific mental states. For instance:

a. Alpha waves: Associated with calm and relaxation.
      b. Beta waves: Linked to focus, concentration, and cognitive activity.
      c. Theta waves: Related to drowsiness or deep relaxation.
   3. Command Translation: The software maps brainwave patterns to game actions. For example:
      a. Focus harder → Move an object forward.
      b. Relax deeply → Lower an object or unlock a new level.
   4. Game Interaction: The translated signals act as input commands, enabling you to interact with characters, environments, or objects in the game.

Mental States and Game Control

BCI games often use two primary mental states for control:

- Focus and Attention: In these games, maintaining a high level of focus causes actions to happen, such as moving a character forward, lifting an object, or navigating obstacles.
  o Example: Concentrating on an object in the game to make it levitate.
- Relaxation and Calmness: Some BCI games reward players for achieving a relaxed mental state, teaching stress control in the process.
  o Example: Reducing your brainwave activity to calm a storm or solve a puzzle.

These states encourage players to become more aware of their mental activity, enhancing both gameplay and cognitive skills.

Examples of BCI-Controlled Actions in Games

To better understand how brainwaves translate into actions, here are a few examples of BCI mechanics in popular or experimental games:

   1. Movement Control: Players move objects, characters, or

vehicles by maintaining focus or switching between different mental states.
2. Selection and Navigation: Brainwaves control menus or highlight objects for interaction, replacing the need for mouse clicks or button presses.
3. Puzzles and Challenges: Completing tasks by achieving specific brainwave patterns, such as calming your mind to unlock a new path or focusing to build energy for a task.

Real-World Examples of BCI Gaming
- Mind-Controlled Racing Games: Players use focus to accelerate and steer virtual vehicles.
- Meditative Games: The game's environment responds to relaxation levels, such as clearing clouds or calming turbulent waters.
- Brain-Training Games: Designed to improve focus and cognitive functions while offering an engaging experience.

Challenges in BCI Game Control
While BCI games are exciting, they come with challenges:
- Signal Accuracy: Brain signals can be "noisy" due to movement or environmental distractions, requiring players to stay still and focused.
- Learning Curve: Players may need time to master controlling their brainwaves effectively.
- Device Limitations: Consumer EEG headsets, while advanced, still have fewer channels than professional medical-grade devices.

2.4 Hands-On: Beginner-Friendly BCI Games

BCI gaming might sound advanced and intimidating, but in reality, there are beginner-friendly games that allow you to experience the thrill of controlling actions with your brainwaves. This section highlights accessible BCI games, discusses what makes them suitable for beginners, and walks you through how to get started.

What Makes a BCI Game Beginner-Friendly?

For those new to BCI technology, beginner-friendly games share a few common characteristics:

1. Simple Controls: These games rely on basic mental states like focus, relaxation, or simple "on-off" brainwave patterns.
2. Low Learning Curve: They provide immediate feedback to help players quickly understand how their brainwaves influence the game.
3. Short Play Sessions: Beginner-friendly games are often designed for shorter sessions to avoid mental fatigue.
4. Compatibility with Affordable Devices: Most beginner BCI games work seamlessly with consumer-grade EEG headsets like Emotiv Insight and Muse.

Examples of Beginner-Friendly BCI Games

1. MindLift (Focus-Based Game)
   a. Description: A simple yet engaging game that requires players to focus intensely to lift objects on the screen. As your focus level increases, objects move higher or faster, providing immediate feedback.
   b. How It Works: Players learn to maintain a state of high beta wave activity (associated with focus and concentration) to control objects.
   c. Why It's Beginner-Friendly: The visual feedback is clear and immediate, helping players practice and fine-tune their focus.
2. The Mind Labyrinth (Relaxation Game)
   a. Description: This meditative game immerses players in a calming virtual environment where their relaxation state helps solve puzzles or progress through levels.
   b. How It Works: Achieving deeper states of

relaxation (low alpha and theta waves) allows you to unlock pathways, calm storms, or illuminate dark areas.
      c. Why It's Beginner-Friendly: It introduces players to relaxation-based controls in an intuitive, stress-free way.
   3. BrainDriver (Racing Game)
      a. Description: A fun, interactive racing game where focus levels control the car's speed. The more focused you are, the faster your car moves. Losing focus causes the car to slow down or stop.
      b. How It Works: The game measures beta wave activity for focus and attention and maps it to the car's speed.
      c. Why It's Beginner-Friendly: It combines competition and entertainment with simple brainwave control mechanics.
   4. ZenZone (Mindfulness and Stress Relief)
      a. Description: ZenZone encourages players to relax deeply by presenting nature-inspired environments that respond to relaxation levels, such as clearing fog or calming waves.
      b. How It Works: Relaxation states (high alpha, low beta) cause the game environment to become peaceful and serene.
      c. Why It's Beginner-Friendly: It's perfect for those new to BCI gaming who want to develop mindfulness skills while having fun.

How to Get Started with Beginner BCI Games
   1. Choose the Right Headset: Use an EEG device like Emotiv Insight or Muse, as these are affordable and compatible with many beginner-friendly games.
   2. Install Software and Apps: Most games have dedicated software or apps that connect your EEG headset to the

game. Follow the provided instructions for setup.
3. Set Clear Goals: Decide what you want to practice —focus, relaxation, or simply experimenting with brainwave control.
4. Start Small: Begin with short sessions (10–15 minutes) to avoid mental fatigue and gradually build up as you become comfortable.
5. Track Your Progress: Many games offer built-in tracking tools that help you see your improvements over time. Use these to adjust your strategies.

Why Start with These Games?
Beginner-friendly BCI games are not only fun but also help you build confidence in using EEG devices. They provide a solid foundation for understanding how your brainwaves work, teaching you to consciously control focus or relaxation states—skills that can later be applied to more advanced games or even real-life scenarios.

Step-by-Step Tutorial: Getting Started with BCI-Controlled Games
This tutorial walks readers through using a BCI headset to play beginner-friendly brain-controlled games.

Step 1: Set Up Your BCI Device
1. Power on your BCI headset (e.g., Emotiv Insight or Muse).
2. Connect it to your computer, tablet, or smartphone via Bluetooth or USB cable as instructed by the device manual.
3. Ensure all sensors are in proper contact with your scalp for accurate readings. Calibration may be required — follow the device app prompts to complete this process.

Step 2: Choose a Beginner-Friendly BCI Game
Start with simple brain-controlled games to familiarize yourself

with how BCI works. Examples include:

- Mind Pong: A classic game where you use focus (Beta waves) to move a paddle up or down.
- Attention Trainer: A game that rewards sustained focus to complete challenges like moving objects on the screen.
- Relax-to-Win: A game where you calm your mind (increasing Alpha waves) to progress in the game, such as growing a tree or flowing water.

Download these games or apps compatible with your BCI headset. Examples include EmotivBCI, Brain Trainer, or Muse Calm.

Step 3: Calibrate Your Brainwaves for the Game
1. Launch the game and follow its calibration instructions. Most beginner games will prompt you to "focus" or "relax" to train the system to recognize your Beta or Alpha waves.
2. For focus games: Stare at an object or think about a single thought while maintaining high attention levels.
3. For relaxation games: Breathe slowly and deeply while clearing your mind.

The game will adjust sensitivity to your brainwave signals during calibration.

Step 4: Play the Game
1. Start the game and observe how your brainwaves affect gameplay. For example:
    a. In Mind Pong, your paddle moves when you increase focus.
    b. In Relax-to-Win, progress occurs when Alpha waves are dominant.
2. Pay attention to moments of success or failure. Were you fully focused or distracted? Make mental notes on what triggers your brainwave patterns.

Step 5: Reflect and Practice
After gameplay:
- Review feedback provided by the app or EEG software. For example, did you maintain steady Beta waves for focus or Alpha waves for relaxation?
- Practice regularly to improve control over your brainwaves. With time, you'll notice increased consistency in gameplay and mental state control.

2.5 Training Your Brain for Better Control

Using a BCI to play games effectively requires practice and consistency, much like developing any other skill. This section will guide you through techniques and exercises to train your brain for better control over BCI devices.

1. Understanding Brain-Training Basics
    a. BCI games rely on your brain's ability to produce clear and consistent signals that the headset can interpret. For most users, this means learning to focus, stay calm, and avoid distractions during gameplay. This is a skill that develops over time with practice.
2. Focus and Relaxation Exercises
    a. Breathing Techniques: Before starting a BCI game, spend five minutes practicing slow, deep breathing. This can help you reach a calm state of mind, reducing "noise" in your brainwaves that might interfere with the BCI's ability to read your signals.
    b. Meditative Focus: Spend a few minutes focusing on one simple thought or image. This will help you practice controlling your mind's activity, which is essential for consistent gameplay.
3. Step-by-Step Training Process
    a. Begin with simple activities to familiarize yourself with the device:

i. Start Small: Use beginner-friendly BCI games that only require basic signals, like focusing or relaxing to move objects on the screen.
b. Set Goals: Establish small, manageable milestones for signal control, like increasing your ability to sustain focus for ten seconds. Gradually work toward longer durations.
c. Track Progress: Many BCI devices offer data or feedback on how well your brain signals are being interpreted. Use this information to identify where you struggle and improve over time.

4. Common Challenges and How to Overcome Them
    a. Many new users face challenges when training with BCI devices:
        i. Inconsistent Signals: If your brainwaves are inconsistent, it's often due to stress, fatigue, or multitasking. Address this by resting and improving focus before sessions.
    b. Frustration: It can be frustrating when the BCI doesn't respond as expected. Stay patient, take breaks, and return with a calm mindset. Improvement takes time.

5. Advanced Control Techniques
    a. As you gain confidence, experiment with more advanced techniques:
        i. Visualization: Use mental imagery to strengthen specific brainwave patterns. For instance, imagine a calm lake to generate relaxation signals or a moving object to boost focus.
        ii. Multi-Signal Control: Some BCI

devices allow you to train multiple signals simultaneously (e.g., focus and relaxation). Practice switching between mental states for more nuanced control.

By consistently applying these techniques, you'll develop greater mastery over your BCI device. Training your brain takes dedication, but the results will lead to a far more engaging and rewarding BCI gaming experience.

2.6 Advanced Techniques for BCI Gaming

Once you've mastered the basics of using BCI devices for gaming, you can begin exploring advanced strategies to improve precision, control, and overall gameplay. This section will introduce techniques that can elevate your skills to a higher level.

1. Combining Mental States for Multi-Level Control

Advanced BCI games often require more than one mental state for input, such as focus, relaxation, or visualization.

- Simultaneous Signals: Practice generating two distinct signals, such as deep relaxation while maintaining a focused thought. This allows for more complex actions, like navigating or multitasking within the game.
- Switching States Quickly: Train yourself to rapidly transition between mental states (e.g., switching from calm relaxation to focused concentration), which can help in games requiring quick reflexes or fast decision-making.

2. Fine-Tuning Brainwave Patterns

- Signal Precision: Work on producing clean, consistent brainwave signals by focusing on specific thoughts or imagery. Use your BCI feedback to observe how your signals respond and adjust accordingly.
- Mental Conditioning: Treat BCI control like athletic training. Short, focused sessions over time will help condition your

brain to generate specific wave patterns reliably.
- Biofeedback Integration: Many BCI devices now offer visual or auditory biofeedback tools that help you observe your brain activity in real-time. Use these tools to refine your control.

3. Gamifying Brain Training
Advanced users can create challenges and systems to keep brain training engaging:

- Time Challenges: Set goals to improve response times or maintain focus for longer durations. For example, sustaining focus for thirty seconds could unlock new levels of control.
- High-Precision Tasks: Select BCI games or tools that require finer control, such as guiding small objects through tight spaces or performing actions with minimal input.

4. Visualization and Mental Imagery Mastery
Advanced BCI gaming often relies heavily on visualization techniques to generate specific brainwave activity.

- Complex Imagery: Visualize more detailed mental images (e.g., imagine steering a car on a winding road or balancing an object). This sharpens the brain's ability to produce targeted signals.
- Active Visualization: Practice combining visualizations with mental commands to improve coordination and control within the game.

5. Integrating Physical and Cognitive Training
For peak performance, combine your brain training with cognitive and physical exercises:

- Cognitive Workouts: Use puzzles, strategy games, or memory challenges alongside BCI training to strengthen overall brain performance.
- Physical Relaxation Techniques: Use yoga, stretching, or deep breathing to calm the body while maintaining mental focus —this can enhance signal clarity.

6. Customizing Your BCI Setup
Advanced BCI gamers may need to tweak their setup to achieve optimal performance:

- Adjusting Sensitivity: Fine-tune your BCI device settings to ensure the system is highly responsive to your brainwave patterns.
- Experimenting with Tools: Pair your BCI headset with software that offers advanced data tracking and analysis, helping you better understand how to improve your signals.

7. Creating a Long-Term Training Plan
Just like elite athletes, advanced BCI users benefit from structured, long-term training:

- Weekly Goals: Set weekly milestones for signal precision, reaction speed, or sustained focus.
- Review Progress: Use EEG feedback to track improvements and identify areas for growth.
- Balance Practice and Recovery: Avoid overtraining, as mental fatigue can weaken your signals. Include rest days to allow your brain to recover and strengthen.

By incorporating these advanced techniques, you'll refine your BCI skills and unlock new possibilities in BCI gaming. As you continue training, you'll not only gain greater control but also enhance your ability to push the boundaries of what's possible with brainwave-powered gameplay.

2.7 Case Studies: The Power of BCI Gaming
This section highlights real-world examples of how BCI gaming has transformed the way individuals interact with technology, enhancing their gaming experiences, cognitive abilities, and even quality of life. These case studies provide concrete illustrations of the potential impact of BCI devices.

1. Enhancing Reaction Time and Focus in Competitive Gaming

Case Study: Sam, an Aspiring eSports Player

Sam, a young gamer aiming to break into competitive eSports, struggled with maintaining focus during high-stakes matches. He began using a consumer-grade BCI headset to train his brain to sustain focus and improve reaction times.

Training Approach: Sam used focus-based BCI games to condition his brain to remain in a state of peak concentration. By tracking his EEG data, he identified mental patterns that allowed him to maintain steady focus under pressure.

Results: Within three months, Sam's reaction time improved by twenty percent, and his ability to stay engaged for extended periods increased significantly. His enhanced focus helped him perform better in competitive settings, moving him closer to his professional goals.

2. Overcoming Cognitive Fatigue for Long Gaming Sessions
Case Study: Alex, a Streamer Balancing Gaming and Mental Well-Being

Alex, a gaming content creator who streams for hours daily, faced frequent mental fatigue and reduced performance over long sessions. Introducing EEG-based tools into his routine allowed him to monitor his brain states and implement better strategies for recovery.

Training Approach: Alex used relaxation-focused BCI exercises between streaming sessions to regulate stress and mental strain. He also tracked his brainwave patterns to identify when his cognitive performance started declining.

Results: Alex learned to take short, targeted breaks when his EEG data indicated fatigue. This improved his endurance, reduced burnout, and increased the quality of his gameplay for audiences.

3. Improving Accessibility in Gaming for Individuals with

Disabilities
Case Study: Maria, a Gamer with Limited Mobility

Maria, an avid gamer with a physical disability that limited her hand movement, explored BCI gaming as a new way to engage with her favorite hobby. Using a BCI headset with a mental control game, she trained her brain to issue commands without physical input.

Training Approach: Maria started with beginner-friendly BCI games that relied on simple mental states like focus and relaxation. Over time, she developed the ability to issue precise, multi-command inputs using visualization techniques.

Results: BCI gaming provided Maria with a new level of freedom and accessibility. She was able to compete in games that once seemed out of reach, empowering her to reconnect with the gaming community.

4. Boosting Brain Performance Through Gamified Training
Case Study: Kevin, a Student and Casual Gamer

Kevin, a university student, wanted to use gaming not only for recreation but also for improving his cognitive skills. He integrated EEG-powered brain training games into his daily routine.

Training Approach: Kevin used BCI software that focused on improving attention, memory, and mental agility. He combined brainwave exercises with academic study sessions to maximize productivity.

Results: Kevin noticed marked improvements in his ability to focus during study sessions and retain information. His brain training through BCI gaming translated into both better academic performance and enhanced gameplay.

5. Exploring New Levels of Immersion in Gaming

Case Study: Sarah, a VR Enthusiast Exploring BCI Integration

Sarah, a technology enthusiast and VR gamer, wanted a deeper level of immersion in her virtual environments. By pairing her VR headset with a BCI device, she began experimenting with brainwave control in VR games.

Training Approach: Sarah practiced using her brain signals to perform actions in VR worlds, such as manipulating objects, navigating environments, and interacting with game elements.

Results: The combination of VR and BCI provided an unprecedented sense of immersion for Sarah. She described feeling like her mind was directly connected to the game world, creating a more intuitive and satisfying gaming experience.

6. Empowering Gamers with Disabilities
Case Study: Jake, a 28-year-old gamer

Jake was diagnosed with a neuromuscular condition that limited his ability to use traditional gaming controllers. Determined to play, Jake adopted an EEG-based BCI headset, the Emotiv Insight, as an alternative input tool.

Implementation: Using brainwave signals, Jake mapped simple mental states to in-game actions—relaxing his mind for forward movement and focusing sharply for specific commands like shooting or pausing. Over time, Jake practiced controlling his brainwaves with consistency.

Results: After six months of dedicated training. Jake successfully played competitive FPS games with accuracy comparable to traditional players. He inspired a small community of gamers with physical disabilities to explore EEG devices for accessibility.

Key Insight: EEG-controlled gaming can unlock new opportunities for individuals with physical limitations, empowering them to enjoy immersive gaming experiences.

7. Improving Reaction Time in Esports

Case Study: Sarah, a competitive esports player

Sara specialized in real-time strategy (RTS) games and struggled with delayed reaction times and mental fatigue during tournaments. To address this, she incorporated an EEG-based Muse headset into her training routine.

Implementation: Sarah focused on:
Real-time EEG feedback to identify moments of distraction.
Reaction-time drills designed to enhance focus and reduce cognitive latency.
Post-session EEG analysis to identify points of stress and fatigue during gameplay.

Results: Over three months of EEG-focused training:
Sarah improved her response time by 15% and stayed mentally sharper during high-pressure tournaments. EEG techniques became a core part of her team's esports preparation strategy.

Key Insight: EEG devices provide measurable data to fine-tune focus and reaction time, giving competitive gamers a significant edge.

8. The Future of EEG in VR Gaming

Case Study: A glimpse into the year 2030 reveals a fully immersive VR game controlled entirely by brainwave signals using advanced EEG-based BCI headsets. Players no longer rely on controllers or gestures—brain activity directs all interactions.

Implementation: A calm brainwave state enables smooth motion (walking, flying) in the virtual world. Focus and clarity trigger object interactions, solving puzzles, or executing combat strategies. EEG data dynamically personalizes the environment—calming visuals appear if stress levels spike.

Results: Players experience unprecedented levels of immersion, as brainwave control seamlessly integrates with the VR game.

EEG data enhances both performance and emotional engagement, making gaming intuitive and hyper-personalized.

Key Insight: EEG-controlled VR gaming showcases the immense potential of BCI technology to redefine interactivity and immersion in future digital experiences.

These case studies showcase the versatility of BCI gaming, whether it's improving reaction time for competitive players, increasing accessibility for individuals with disabilities, or unlocking entirely new ways to interact with virtual worlds. By leveraging brainwave technology, gamers of all backgrounds can enhance their performance, explore innovative gaming experiences, and push the boundaries of what's possible in interactive entertainment.

Interviews with Experts or Insights from Gamers
To add more depth and credibility, this section introduces real-world insights from gamers who have used EEG and BCI technology to enhance their gaming experiences, along with thoughts from experts in neurotechnology.

Gamer's Perspective on BCI Control
Name: Alex Turner, Competitive Gamer

Background: Alex is an esports player who began experimenting with BCI technology to improve reaction time and gaming strategy.

Insight:
"I started using BCI tools with games like Brain Pong just out of curiosity. Initially, I struggled to calibrate my brainwaves, but once I got the hang of focusing and relaxing on command, it became a game-changer—literally. EEG training helped me become more aware of my mental state, and I noticed a huge boost in my focus during tournaments. It's like learning to control your brain as much as your physical actions, and the awareness

transfers to every game I play."

Takeaway: Gamers can train their minds to maintain intense focus and improve reaction speeds using EEG and BCI tools. The technology not only enhances performance but also teaches mental resilience under pressure.

Expert Insight: Neurofeedback and the Gaming Industry
Name: Dr. Emily Lin, Cognitive Neuroscientist

Background: Dr. Lin is a researcher specializing in brain-computer interfaces and their application in interactive technologies.

Insight:
"BCI tools are pushing the boundaries of gaming by blending cognitive science and entertainment. EEG-based neurofeedback systems are helping gamers understand their brainwave states, offering a unique edge in mental performance. For casual players, the technology makes gaming more immersive; for professionals, it provides an unprecedented way to train focus and mental endurance. While still evolving, the potential for EEG in gaming is massive."

Takeaway: EEG and BCI technologies are not just for researchers —they are tools gamers can use to improve performance and unlock new opportunities. Experts anticipate a future where EEG-integrated games become a mainstream tool for both entertainment and brain training.

2.8 Future Possibilities: The Evolution of EEG and BCI in Gaming

The future of EEG and BCI technology in gaming is full of potential, offering exciting opportunities for gamers, developers, and researchers alike. As technology advances, the gaming industry is poised to unlock new levels of immersion, accessibility, and personal performance enhancement. This section explores emerging trends, innovations, and the possibilities on the horizon.

1. Fully Immersive Brain-Controlled Gaming

With the rapid development of EEG and BCI technology, the dream of fully brain-controlled games is closer than ever. Future advancements may allow gamers to interact with virtual environments entirely through brain signals, eliminating the need for traditional controllers or physical inputs.

- Imagine navigating a complex virtual world, solving puzzles, or competing in battles simply by thinking about your actions. EEG signals could replace conventional input devices, enabling a seamless mind-to-game connection.
- This level of immersion will create personalized gaming experiences where emotional and cognitive states influence gameplay, such as games that adjust their difficulty based on a player's stress or focus levels.

2. Integration of EEG and BCI with VR and AR

The combination of EEG/BCI with VR and AR has the potential to redefine the gaming experience. By merging brainwave technology with immersive visuals and environments, players will engage with games on a deeper, more intuitive level.

In VR, brain-controlled actions could enable precise movement, mental manipulation of objects, and tailored environments that respond to a player's mental states. AR could use EEG signals to enhance focus and decision-making in real-world applications, turning everyday activities into gamified experiences.

3. Enhanced Personalization through Brainwave Feedback

Future games may leverage real-time EEG data to create adaptive and personalized gaming experiences. By continuously monitoring brainwaves, games can adjust their mechanics, visuals, and challenges to match the player's cognitive and emotional states.

For example, a game might detect when a player is becoming

fatigued or frustrated and adjust the pace or difficulty to keep engagement high. Similarly, games could adapt music, lighting, and gameplay dynamics to induce calm, focus, or excitement, optimizing the experience for each player.

4. Brainwave-Driven eSports and Competitive Gaming

As EEG devices become more sophisticated, brainwave monitoring may play a significant role in professional eSports. Advanced tools could allow players to optimize their mental states for peak performance, offering a competitive edge.

Gamers may use EEG-based biofeedback to train their focus, improve reaction times, and regulate stress under high-pressure conditions. Professional tournaments could include brainwave metrics as part of performance analysis, evaluating players' mental agility alongside their physical gameplay.

5. Accessibility and Inclusion in Gaming

One of the most promising possibilities for EEG and BCI in gaming is the potential to make games more accessible to players with physical disabilities. By eliminating the need for manual controls, brainwave technology opens doors for individuals who have traditionally faced barriers in gaming.

Advanced BCI systems may empower players to fully control games with their minds, offering more intuitive interfaces and interactions.

Developers are already exploring inclusive design solutions, ensuring that future EEG-powered games are accessible to players of all abilities.

6. Cognitive Training Platforms with Gamification

Beyond entertainment, EEG and BCI could transform gaming into a tool for cognitive development. Future games may focus on training specific mental skills, such as memory, attention, and stress management, through fun and engaging experiences.

Gamified brain training could appeal to students, professionals, and casual players looking to enhance their mental performance. EEG data could track progress over time, providing measurable insights into improvements in focus, reaction speed, and cognitive resilience.

7. AI and Machine Learning Integration
The integration of Artificial Intelligence (AI) and Machine Learning (ML) with EEG and BCI systems could significantly enhance their capabilities. AI could analyze complex brainwave patterns in real time, improving the accuracy and responsiveness of brain-controlled games.

Machine learning algorithms may predict player behavior, adapt gameplay to anticipate cognitive states, and provide smarter feedback loops for improvement. This synergy between AI and EEG technology will push the boundaries of what's possible in gaming.

8. Ethical Considerations and Data Privacy
As EEG and BCI gaming evolves, ethical concerns and data privacy will become increasingly important. Brainwave data is personal and sensitive, raising questions about how this information is collected, stored, and used.

Future developments must prioritize user privacy, ensuring that brainwave data remains secure and under the player's control. Transparent guidelines will be needed to address concerns about how EEG data could be used beyond gaming, such as for marketing or research.

The evolution of EEG and BCI technology promises to reshape the gaming landscape, offering unprecedented opportunities for gamers to interact with their favorite hobby in new and exciting ways. From fully immersive, brain-controlled games to inclusive and personalized experiences, the future is full of innovation. As these advancements unfold, EEG and BCI gaming will continue to push boundaries, inspiring gamers to explore their full cognitive potential while redefining what's possible in interactive entertainment.

FUTURE TRENDS EXPANDED: The Next Frontier for EEG and BCI Gaming

As technology advances, the integration of EEG and BCI in gaming is set to revolutionize not just how we play, but how we interact with technology as a whole. Below are some emerging trends and groundbreaking possibilities to watch in the near future:

1. Hyper-Immersive Virtual Reality (VR) with EEG and BCI

EEG and BCI are being integrated with VR environments to create fully immersive experiences. Imagine playing games where the virtual world reacts to your emotions, mental states, and focus in real-time. A VR adventure game where your focus (Beta waves) helps solve puzzles, while calmness (Alpha waves) influences interactions with the game environment.

2. AI-Powered Brainwave Feedback

Machine learning and artificial intelligence will further personalize EEG-driven gaming experiences. AI algorithms can analyze brainwave data to predict patterns, adjust game difficulty, and provide feedback for real-time brain training. Games will learn your mental strengths and weaknesses, adapting challenges dynamically to improve focus, reaction time, and cognitive endurance.

3. Brain-Controlled Esports and Competitive Gaming

As EEG and BCI tools become more advanced and widely accessible, we may see professional tournaments where players control aspects of the game using only their brainwaves. EEG-enhanced training will also give competitive gamers a cognitive edge. Esports leagues with divisions for brainwave-controlled gaming could open up a new category in the competitive gaming world.

4. EEG Wearables for Continuous Performance Monitoring

Future EEG devices will likely be smaller, more stylish, and easier to wear during long gaming sessions. These headsets will passively collect brainwave data, helping gamers track focus, fatigue, and performance over time. Smart EEG wearables that automatically detect when a player's focus is waning and suggest short neurofeedback exercises to recharge mental clarity.

5. Integration with Haptic Feedback and Other Biofeedback Systems

EEG and BCI systems may merge with haptic feedback devices (wearable technology that simulates touch or movement), creating a multi-sensory gaming experience. When players achieve a certain mental state, haptic feedback can simulate physical sensations, like a pulse of energy or vibrations, to enhance immersion.

6. Brainwave-Driven Open-World Environments

Future games might leverage EEG data to dynamically generate game environments based on your brainwave states. A relaxed mental state might create calm, tranquil game landscapes, while high focus generates more action-packed challenges.

7. Non-Gaming Applications Inspired by EEG Gaming

EEG-driven gaming breakthroughs will likely spill into non-gaming applications, including education, rehabilitation, and workplace productivity. Schools may use EEG-enhanced learning games to improve focus and engagement in students, while workplaces could integrate EEG tools to monitor and optimize mental performance.

8. Accessibility for Disabled Gamers

Brain-computer interfaces hold enormous promise for disabled individuals, enabling hands-free control of games and devices. This technology will unlock new opportunities for inclusivity in gaming. Gamers with physical limitations will be able to compete in and enjoy complex gaming experiences using only their brainwaves.

Final Thoughts on the Future of EEG and BCI Gaming

The future of EEG and BCI in gaming is full of untapped potential. From hyper-immersive virtual reality to AI-driven personalization and accessibility for all, these technologies are redefining the boundaries of gaming. For readers of this book, the skills and knowledge you've gained today can prepare you to become early adopters, pioneers, and even contributors to this exciting evolution. As brainwave technology progresses, so too will the ways in which we play, learn, and connect with the digital world.

2.9 Additional Advanced Techniques and Expanding Your EEG & BCI Skills

For readers who have become comfortable with EEG tools and BCI gaming basics, this section will introduce advanced strategies and creative expansions to push their skills further.

1. Combining EEG with Other Biofeedback Tools
Pair EEG headsets with other biofeedback devices like heart rate variability (HRV) monitors or skin conductance sensors.

Example: Use EEG to monitor focus and HRV to manage stress during gaming. Together, these tools can help optimize physical and mental readiness.

2. Building Custom Brainwave Profiles
Identify specific brainwave patterns that correlate with peak focus, calmness, or reaction times. Work on "anchoring" these states: Practice EEG exercises repeatedly to reinforce your ability to enter these ideal mental zones quickly during gameplay. Advanced tools like EEG Lab or open-source software can allow users to visualize and fine-tune brainwave data.

3. Creating Personalized Training Routines
Develop EEG-focused workouts. Use short, daily sessions to build consistency and improve over time.

Example Routine:

- Morning: 10 minutes of focus exercises to start the day (monitor Beta waves).
- Afternoon: 5 minutes of stress-relief practice (Alpha wave stimulation).
- Evening: 10 minutes of brain-controlled gaming to test mental endurance and focus.

4. Exploring Open-Source BCI Platforms

Platforms like OpenBCI offer greater customization for tech-savvy users. These tools allow advanced users to experiment with more tailored EEG applications, including DIY game controls.

Example Projects: Modifying game interfaces to respond to unique brainwave commands. Building BCI-powered games for practice and entertainment.

5. Pushing BCI Gaming Limits: Multi-Command Control

Train your brain to master multiple brainwave commands for more complex game actions.

Example: Use one brainwave pattern (Alpha) to control movement and another (Beta) to activate special actions in a BCI-compatible game.

6. Experimenting with Machine Learning and EEG

Explore emerging applications where machine learning algorithms analyze EEG data for personalized feedback. Tech enthusiasts can look into integrating EEG tools with Python-based libraries like TensorFlow or BrainFlow to optimize EEG-based tasks.

7. Sharing Your EEG and BCI Journey

Join gaming and neurofeedback communities to share progress, techniques, and new insights. Social platforms like Reddit and Discord often have EEG and BCI enthusiast groups for collaboration.

CHAPTER 3: THE FUTURE OF GAMING WITH EEG

The gaming industry is on the brink of a revolution, and EEG technology is at the heart of it. From Augmented Reality (AR) to Artificial Intelligence (AI), the integration of brainwave technology into gaming is reshaping what's possible. Imagine a world where your focus adjusts the difficulty of a game in real-time, or where fully immersive environments respond to your emotions and thoughts. These innovations are no longer futuristic dreams—they're becoming a reality.

In this chapter, we'll explore how EEG technology is driving the future of gaming. You'll learn about the synergy between brainwaves and cutting-edge technologies like Virtual Reality (VR), AR, and AI. We'll also dive into emerging trends, from adaptive gaming experiences to fully immersive brain-controlled environments. Whether you're a gamer, developer, or innovator, this chapter will inspire you to see how EEG can redefine the gaming landscape and push the boundaries of human potential.

3.1 Brainwaves and Virtual Reality (VR)

VR has revolutionized gaming by immersing players in hyper-realistic digital worlds. But what happens when we combine the immersive power of VR with EEG brainwave technology? The result is a completely new frontier of gameplay—one where players don't just interact with a game but actually control it using their minds.

How EEG Integrates with VR
EEG headsets can monitor brainwave patterns in real time and translate those signals into specific game actions. In a VR environment, these signals can control movements, trigger events, or even alter the game world based on the player's mental state. For example:

- Thought-Based Movement: Players can move their avatars or interact with objects using mental focus instead of handheld controllers.
- Emotional Feedback Loops: Games can adapt to your emotional state—calming visuals when you're stressed, or high-intensity challenges when your focus peaks.
- Immersive Training: EEG-enabled VR can help gamers practice skills like focus, reaction time, and stress management in hyper-realistic scenarios.

Real-World Applications
The combination of EEG and VR isn't just theoretical—early applications are already emerging:

1. Mind-Controlled VR Games: Experimental games allow players to move characters or complete tasks by concentrating on specific mental cues.
2. Immersive Biofeedback: Games designed for relaxation use EEG to monitor brain activity and immerse the player in calming environments tailored to their brainwaves.
3. Mental Focus Challenges: VR worlds where progression relies on maintaining high focus levels. For example, platforms or doors might unlock only when your

brainwaves hit a focus threshold.

Why This Matters for Gamers
Integrating EEG and VR unlocks new levels of immersion and interactivity:

- Gamers can enhance their cognitive skills while playing—training focus, mental clarity, and reaction time.
- VR experiences become more adaptive and personalized, responding dynamically to how a player thinks and feels.
- Competitive gaming evolves, as players who harness their brainwaves effectively will have a real advantage.

Future Possibilities
Looking ahead, the possibilities are boundless:

- Mind-Controlled Avatars: Entire VR universes could be navigated solely through brainwave input, eliminating the need for controllers.
- Adaptive VR Worlds: Environments that change in real time based on your brain activity—calming when you're stressed or intensifying when you're engaged.
- Hybrid Gaming and Training: EEG-VR games designed to boost real-world skills like focus, stress resilience, and cognitive control while still offering immersive fun.

This integration of VR and EEG is still in its infancy, but it's clear that the combination has the potential to redefine the gaming experience as we know it. For gamers, this means getting ready to step into a world where the boundaries between thought and action are blurred—where your mind becomes your ultimate controller.

3.2 Augmented Reality (AR) Meets EEG

AR overlays digital elements onto the real world, blending physical and virtual environments into a seamless experience. Now, when AR is combined with EEG brainwave technology, the result is a powerful new way for gamers to interact with their surroundings—using their minds as the bridge between reality and the game.

How EEG Integrates with AR

EEG headsets monitor brain activity, capturing signals such as focus, relaxation, and mental engagement. These signals are then fed into AR systems to interact with virtual elements in real-time. Some potential ways EEG and AR combine include:

- Thought-Controlled Overlays: Users can manipulate AR objects or environments using mental focus. For example, a player could use brainwaves to "lift" virtual objects or unlock AR doors.
- Mental State-Driven Environments: The AR experience adapts to your cognitive state, providing hints or changing challenges based on how focused or calm you are.
- Enhanced Real-Time Feedback: AR visuals could display brainwave data directly in the player's field of view, such as focus levels, progress tracking, or mental state metrics.

Examples of EEG and AR in Action

While still emerging, EEG-AR technology has already begun to show its potential:

1. Interactive AR Games: Simple AR games now incorporate EEG, where focus controls character actions, and relaxation unlocks new areas. Imagine a game where hitting a "focus threshold" reveals hidden clues in your real-world surroundings.
2. Cognitive Training Tools: AR environments designed for mental training could display tasks in real life that respond to your brainwave input. For instance, puzzles or focus challenges might get harder as your brain improves.
3. Immersive Education and Learning: Gamers using EEG headsets could explore AR worlds that adapt to their level of focus and engagement—helping to learn

skills like strategy, pattern recognition, or real-world problem-solving.

Why AR + EEG is Important for Gamers
Combining EEG with AR enhances gaming in several key ways:

- Hands-Free Gameplay: By removing the need for physical controls, EEG allows for a more fluid and intuitive interaction with AR elements.
- Personalized Challenges: Games can adjust to each player's cognitive abilities, creating a tailored experience that pushes their mental boundaries.
- Enhanced Immersion: AR games become more dynamic, reacting not only to physical movement but also to your thoughts and emotions.

For example, in AR-based strategy games, a player's mental focus could "reveal" enemies in their surroundings, while calm and clear thinking could trigger power-ups or bonuses. This creates an environment where gamers are rewarded for improving cognitive skills in a way that directly influences their success in the game.

Future Possibilities
As EEG and AR technologies advance, the future offers incredible possibilities:

- Augmented Mental Workouts: AR apps that integrate EEG could train players to maintain focus under pressure by overlaying mental challenges in real-world settings.
- Real-World Gamification: Everyday environments (e.g., your home, office, or city streets) could be transformed into AR games that respond to your brain activity.
- Mixed Reality Adventures: Combining EEG with AR and VR would create hybrid experiences where gamers shift between digital and physical worlds using nothing but their minds.

A New Level of Interaction
Augmented Reality already blurs the line between virtual and real,

but EEG pushes it further. By combining brainwave control with AR, gamers can turn everyday life into an interactive adventure, training their cognitive abilities while enjoying immersive gameplay. In short, the mind becomes the ultimate tool for shaping augmented worlds, offering a glimpse into the next generation of gaming.

3.3 AI and Adaptive Gaming with EEG

AI and EEG brainwave technology are transforming gaming into a more intelligent, personalized, and adaptive experience. By analyzing brainwave data in real time, AI can tailor gameplay to a gamer's unique mental state—creating a dynamic, ever-evolving challenge that enhances both immersion and skill development.

How AI Enhances EEG in Gaming

AI algorithms excel at analyzing vast amounts of data, and EEG brainwaves provide valuable input about a player's mental activity. Here's how they work together:

- Real-Time Adaptation: AI detects brainwave patterns such as focus, stress, or fatigue and automatically adjusts game difficulty, pace, or objectives. If a player is too stressed, AI might lower the challenge to encourage relaxation.
- Personalized Gaming: Using EEG data, AI learns a player's behavior and cognitive strengths, crafting personalized challenges to improve focus, reaction times, or mental resilience.
- Predictive Insights: AI can anticipate a player's performance based on brainwave trends and suggest actionable strategies to optimize their mental state for better gameplay.

Key Applications of AI and EEG in Gaming

1. Adaptive Difficulty Systems: AI monitors EEG data to determine when a player is overly stressed or disengaged. For instance:
    a. If stress levels spike, AI might slow down

enemy attacks or offer hints.
   b. If focus drops, the game could provide smaller, manageable goals to re-engage the player.
2. Cognitive Skill Training: AI-driven EEG games act as brain training tools. For example:
   a. Focus Challenges: AI increases task complexity as brainwave data shows improving concentration.
   b. Reaction Time Tasks: AI uses real-time EEG signals to refine timing and responsiveness, helping players sharpen their reactions.
3. Dynamic Game Storytelling: EEG and AI can alter the storyline or in-game events based on emotional states. Imagine a role-playing game where the plot adapts to your stress, excitement, or calmness—making each playthrough a unique, responsive experience.
4. AI-Powered Brainwave Insights: AI analyzes EEG sessions to provide feedback on performance. For instance:
   a. Focus tracking graphs might reveal when players performed their best.
   b. Stress heat maps could show areas of the game that triggered mental fatigue.

The Benefits of Adaptive AI Gaming

The fusion of AI and EEG offers significant benefits for gamers:

- Enhanced Engagement: Games remain challenging but not overwhelming, as AI balances difficulty in real time.
- Skill Development: AI tailors exercises to boost focus, speed, and cognitive resilience, turning gameplay into a training ground for mental growth.
- Immersive Experience: Dynamic storylines and environments adapt seamlessly to players' brain activity, enhancing emotional connection and immersion.

For example, a competitive esports player might use EEG with

AI-powered insights to analyze their focus zones during critical gameplay. The AI would identify patterns and suggest strategies like mental breaks or breathing exercises to optimize their future performance.

AI and EEG in Multiplayer Gaming
Adaptive gaming doesn't stop at single-player experiences. In multiplayer scenarios, AI and EEG can enhance collaboration and competition:

- Team Syncing: AI could analyze brainwave data across a team, ensuring all members are mentally aligned before critical in-game moments.
- Competitive Edge: Players might use EEG-driven insights to identify weaknesses in their performance and adapt their playstyle dynamically.

Imagine a multiplayer battle arena where teams with better focus—tracked through EEG—unlock bonuses or gain the upper hand, blending mental performance with strategy.

The Future of AI and EEG Gaming
As technology advances, the possibilities for AI and EEG integration will continue to grow:

- AI Coaches: Virtual AI coaches could monitor players' brainwaves and provide real-time feedback to boost performance.
- Emotionally Intelligent Games: Future games might react to a player's emotional state, adjusting visuals, sounds, and challenges to optimize enjoyment and engagement.
- Long-Term Performance Analysis: AI could provide a "brain profile," tracking cognitive improvements over months or years, helping gamers measure their growth in focus, reaction time, and resilience.

A New Era of Gaming
AI and EEG are unlocking unprecedented possibilities for

adaptive gaming, where the game evolves alongside the player. This cutting-edge combination ensures that gamers are not just entertained—they are continuously challenged, learning, and improving, all while enjoying an immersive and personalized experience.

3.4 The Future: Integrating EEG into Full-Immersion Gaming

The future of gaming is rapidly moving toward full-immersion experiences, where EEG technology will play a pivotal role in creating unprecedented levels of engagement, control, and realism. As VR, AR, and brainwave monitoring converge, gamers will experience fully interactive worlds shaped by their mental and emotional states.

What is Full-Immersion Gaming?

Full-immersion gaming seeks to completely integrate the player's physical, mental, and emotional presence into the game. Technologies like VR headsets, motion sensors, haptic feedback suits, and now EEG brainwave devices are key components in creating this immersive experience. EEG will serve as the bridge between the gamer's mind and the game, blurring the lines between thought and action.

EEG's Role in Full Immersion

EEG brainwave devices will transform immersion by allowing games to respond to brain signals in real time. This means games will adapt, interact, and evolve based on the player's cognitive and emotional states. Here's how EEG will drive this evolution:

- Direct Mental Control: EEG devices will allow players to move objects, control environments, or perform in-game actions simply by focusing or altering their brainwave patterns.
- Adaptive Environments: Imagine an RPG where the weather, lighting, or enemy behavior shifts based on your stress or relaxation levels. If the game detects focus, it could open

hidden paths or unlock challenging puzzles.
- Emotion-Driven Storylines: EEG data can shape the game's narrative. For instance, if a player feels excited, the game may amplify action sequences. If stress is detected, the storyline might shift to more meditative, calm environments.

EEG + VR/AR: Creating a "Living" Game World

Combining EEG with virtual or augmented reality opens up groundbreaking possibilities:

1. Thought-Based Navigation: In VR environments, players could navigate landscapes or interact with objects using their brainwaves instead of controllers. A relaxed state might allow smooth flying, while intense focus activates combat movements.
2. Immersive AR Layers: In augmented reality, EEG could adapt the digital overlays placed on the real world. For instance, focusing on a virtual puzzle in an AR game might make it "come alive," interacting directly with the player's attention.
3. Total Cognitive Feedback: Full-immersion games will continuously monitor players' brainwaves, adjusting difficulty and engagement to keep them in the flow state —the perfect balance of challenge and focus.

The Impact on Gaming Experiences

Here's what full-immersion EEG gaming could look like:

- Hyper-Personalization: Every gamer's brainwave data is unique, meaning every experience will be customized. The game will "learn" how you think and adapt in real time.
- Stress and Focus Modes: EEG could allow players to toggle between stress-relief modes for relaxation and high-performance modes to enhance focus during competitive play.
- Physical and Mental Integration: Pairing EEG with physical inputs—like motion sensors or haptics—will create

experiences where mental and physical skills work together seamlessly.

For example, in a full-immersion racing game, EEG might detect when a player becomes overstimulated during high speeds. The game could automatically slow the visuals while maintaining the adrenaline rush, ensuring players remain focused and engaged.

Challenges and Opportunities
While integrating EEG into full-immersion gaming is promising, challenges remain:

- Technology Accessibility: High-quality EEG devices still need to become affordable and user-friendly for mainstream adoption.
- Calibration and Accuracy: Games will require fine-tuned EEG algorithms to avoid misinterpreting brain signals.
- Ethics and Privacy: Brainwave data is highly personal, so ensuring ethical usage and data privacy will be crucial.

Despite these challenges, companies are already exploring EEG's role in immersive technologies. As EEG devices become more affordable and VR/AR systems continue to evolve, gamers can expect a more responsive, personalized, and immersive experience than ever before.

The Road Ahead
The fusion of EEG, VR, AR, and AI will lead gaming into an exciting future where the boundaries of reality are pushed further than ever before. Gamers won't just play—they will live inside the game, using their minds to shape worlds, solve challenges, and achieve levels of focus and control previously unimaginable.

Full-immersion EEG gaming isn't a distant dream. It's the natural evolution of interactive entertainment, and it holds the promise of transforming the gaming industry into something deeply personal, mentally stimulating, and endlessly engaging.

3.5 Community and Collaboration

Engaging with a community of like-minded individuals can significantly enhance your journey with EEG and gaming. The growth of interest in brain-computer interfaces and gaming has fostered a vibrant and supportive community. By joining these spaces, you not only gain valuable insights but also connect with others who share your curiosity and passion.

Start by exploring online forums and social media groups dedicated to EEG devices and gaming innovations. Platforms like Reddit have active subreddits where members share tips, experiences, and challenges related to EEG and gaming. Discord servers often host niche communities where gamers, developers, and researchers collaborate in real time.

Consider attending virtual or in-person meetups, workshops, or conferences. Events like the NeuroGaming Conference and Expo or webinars hosted by EEG device manufacturers are excellent opportunities to learn and network. These spaces allow you to engage with industry leaders, developers, and enthusiasts.

If you're a developer or gamer looking to innovate, these communities often provide a wealth of inspiration. Collaborations can lead to groundbreaking projects or even the creation of entirely new gaming genres. For instance, sharing ideas about EEG applications can lead to novel game mechanics or improved tools for focus training.

Whether you are seeking technical advice, brainstorming innovative uses for EEG, or simply looking for camaraderie, engaging with the community can transform a solitary pursuit into a shared adventure.

3.6 Ethics Considerations

As the use of EEG technology becomes more prevalent in gaming and beyond, it is essential to address the ethical considerations associated with this innovation. While EEG and brain-computer interfaces (BCIs) open exciting possibilities, they also bring challenges that must be thoughtfully navigated.

One critical area is privacy and data security. EEG devices capture sensitive information about brain activity, which can reveal details about focus, stress levels, and even emotional states. Users and developers alike must prioritize safeguarding this data to prevent misuse or unauthorized access. Always ensure that any platform or device you use complies with data protection standards and allows users to control their own information.

Another key consideration is accessibility and equity. While these technologies offer transformative potential, the cost of EEG devices may limit access for some individuals. Developers and companies should work to create affordable options and consider how to make EEG-related advancements more inclusive.

Additionally, informed consent is vital in any context where EEG data is collected or shared. Users must clearly understand how their data will be used, stored, and shared, particularly in gaming environments where data may be leveraged for AI-driven personalization.

Lastly, it is important to reflect on the impact of EEG-based technologies on mental well-being. While tools for focus and performance enhancement are powerful, over-reliance on such technologies might discourage individuals from cultivating these abilities naturally. It is crucial to strike a balance, viewing EEG as a complement to traditional methods rather than a complete replacement.

CHAPTER 4: OPPORTUNITIES TO MONETIZE EEG AND GAMING INNOVATIONS

The fusion of EEG technology and gaming doesn't just open doors for creative gameplay—it also presents groundbreaking opportunities for innovation and profit. From developing brainwave-powered games to offering training sessions or creating engaging content, the possibilities to monetize this cutting-edge intersection are vast and exciting.

In this chapter, we'll explore how to turn your passion for EEG and gaming into a profitable venture. Whether you're a developer, gamer, or entrepreneur, you'll discover actionable ideas to leverage this technology for financial success. From streaming and affiliate marketing to niche game development and custom EEG setups, this chapter will guide you through strategies to build a business or side hustle around the future of gaming. EEG isn't just about the thrill of playing—it's about creating a thriving ecosystem of innovation and opportunity.

4.1 Developing and Selling BCI-Compatible Games

With the rise of brain-computer interface (BCI) technologies, the gaming industry is evolving toward experiences that use EEG devices to create immersive, brain-controlled gameplay. For those with a knack for development or creativity, there are significant opportunities to build and sell BCI-compatible games, opening up a new frontier in gaming.

How BCI-Compatible Games Work

BCI-compatible games use EEG devices to interpret brain activity, translating it into actionable inputs in the game. For example, focusing your attention could control a character's movement, while relaxation might unlock special abilities. This adds a layer of interactivity that makes gameplay more engaging and futuristic.

Opportunities for Game Developers

Emotiv and other EEG companies provide APIs (Application Programming Interfaces) that developers can use to create games compatible with their devices. For example:

- Emotiv APIs allow developers to access brainwave data in real time, enabling them to create games that respond to mental states like focus, calmness, or excitement.
- Integration Possibilities: These APIs are designed to work seamlessly with popular game engines like Unity and Unreal Engine, making it easier for developers to build unique experiences.

How to Get Started

1. Learn the Tools: Familiarize yourself with EEG devices like Emotiv Insight or Epoc X, and dive into their developer documentation. Start small by integrating brainwave data into existing games or prototyping simple game mechanics.
2. Collaborate with Developers: If you're not a

programmer, consider partnering with game developers who can implement your ideas. Your knowledge of EEG can guide game mechanics that resonate with the device's capabilities.
   3. Target Niche Audiences: Brainwave-controlled games can cater to niche audiences, such as meditation apps for stress relief or competitive esports players looking for an edge.

Monetization Strategies
- Sell Your Game: Publish your game on platforms like Steam, App Store, or Google Play.
- Offer In-App Purchases: Include upgrades or features that players can unlock as they progress.
- License Your Work: License your game concept or EEG integration software to gaming companies interested in entering the BCI space.

4.2 Streaming and Content Creation with EEG and BCI Gaming

EEG and BCI offer exciting opportunities for gamers and content creators to carve out unique niches. From showcasing cutting-edge gameplay to providing educational or entertainment value, EEG and BCI gaming are ideal tools for building an audience and potentially generating income.

Why EEG and BCI Gaming Are Perfect for Streaming
- Novelty Factor: Brain-controlled gaming is still relatively new, which means viewers are drawn to its futuristic appeal and unique mechanics.
- Interactive Appeal: Streaming brainwave data alongside gameplay creates an engaging, educational experience for viewers. They can see how mental focus, relaxation, or excitement directly impact the game.
- Personal Branding: Highlighting your journey as you master BCI gaming makes your content stand out from traditional

gaming streams.

Ideas for Streaming EEG/BCI Gaming
1. Showcase Gameplay: Stream popular BCI-compatible games or demonstrate brainwave-controlled mechanics in real-time.
2. Educational Streams: Teach your audience about brainwaves, how EEG works, and how it's integrated into gaming. Share your setup process, calibration tips, and challenges.
3. Competitive Play: Challenge other BCI gamers to competitions or push for high scores, all while sharing your brainwave data with the audience.
4. Behind-the-Scenes Content: Share how you train your brain for better BCI control or review new EEG devices and games.

Content Ideas Beyond Streaming
- Tutorial Videos: Create "how-to" guides for using EEG devices in gaming, integrating them with platforms like Twitch or YouTube.
- Vlogs: Document your journey of exploring BCI gaming, from beginner frustrations to expert tips.
- Live Q&A: Host live sessions to answer questions about EEG technology, BCI gaming, and how your viewers can get started.

Monetization Strategies
- Ad Revenue: Earn through ad placements on platforms like YouTube or Twitch.
- Sponsorships: Partner with EEG device manufacturers, gaming companies, or tech brands that align with your content.
- Merchandising: Sell branded merchandise like T-shirts, stickers, or posters themed around EEG and BCI gaming.
- Subscriptions: Build a loyal fan base by offering exclusive content or early access through Patreon or platform-specific

memberships.

Tips for Success
- Focus on Consistency: Regularly stream or post content to build and maintain an audience.
- Engage with Viewers: Incorporate interactive elements, like live polls on brainwave performance or audience-chosen challenges.
- Leverage Social Media: Share clips, tips, and behind-the-scenes content on platforms like Instagram, Twitter, or TikTok to attract new viewers.

Streaming and content creation aren't just hobbies—they're powerful tools for sharing the future of gaming while creating a potentially lucrative personal brand. By integrating EEG and BCI gaming into your content, you can stay ahead of trends and captivate audiences eager for innovation.

4.3 Affiliate Marketing with EEG and BCI Gaming

Affiliate marketing offers an excellent opportunity for gamers, educators, and enthusiasts in the EEG and BCI space to earn passive income while promoting cutting-edge tools and technologies. By partnering with EEG device companies, software developers, or other related brands, you can recommend products and services to your audience and earn a commission for each purchase made through your affiliate links.

Why Affiliate Marketing Works for EEG and BCI Gaming
- Niche Market: EEG and BCI devices are still relatively new, which means your audience is likely curious about trustworthy products. Recommending quality tools can establish you as a go-to expert.
- Growing Demand: As the gaming industry continues evolving with brainwave integration, interest in EEG tools, software, and accessories will increase.

- Passive Income: Once you embed affiliate links in videos, blog posts, or descriptions, they can generate income over time without much extra effort.

Ideas for Affiliate Marketing with EEG and BCI Tools

1. EEG Device Recommendations: Partner with companies like Emotiv, Muse, or similar brands to promote their hardware through tutorials, reviews, or live demonstrations.
2. Software or Apps: Promote EEG-compatible games, neurofeedback software, or platforms that support brainwave analysis for gamers.
3. Accessories: Recommend supporting tools, such as VR headsets, gaming gear, or add-ons that complement EEG devices.
4. Guides and Courses: Partner with creators of educational materials or advanced courses that teach others how to use EEG for gaming and performance improvement.

Where to Share Affiliate Links

- Tutorial Videos: Share "how-to" content where you guide viewers through setting up and using EEG devices for gaming.
- Blogs or Articles: Write detailed reviews, comparisons, or guides about EEG tools and BCI-compatible games.
- Live Streams: During EEG or BCI gameplay streams, mention the devices you're using and provide affiliate links in video descriptions.
- Social Media: Post short video clips, infographics, or photos with links directing your followers to products.
- Email Newsletters: Include affiliate links in newsletters highlighting EEG tools, exclusive discounts, or new product launches.

Tips for Successful Affiliate Marketing

1. Promote Products You Believe In: Only recommend

tools and devices you've tested or trust—this builds credibility with your audience.
2. **Be Transparent:** Always disclose affiliate relationships to your audience to maintain trust and comply with guidelines.
3. **Provide Value:** Combine affiliate links with helpful content like tutorials, reviews, or troubleshooting tips.
4. **Negotiate Deals:** Reach out to EEG brands for exclusive discount codes for your audience, giving viewers an incentive to use your links.

Example Affiliate Programs
- Emotiv: Offers referral programs for its EEG headsets and tools.
- Muse: Provides affiliate opportunities for promoting its meditation-focused devices.
- Amazon Associates: A general option where EEG devices, VR gear, and related tools can be linked for commissions.

Affiliate marketing is a low-risk, high-reward strategy for individuals in the EEG and BCI gaming niche. By sharing genuine recommendations and valuable content, you can generate income while helping others explore the benefits of brainwave-powered gaming.

4.4 Game Development for Specific Niches with EEG and BCI Integration

Developing games for specific niches using EEG and BCI technology presents an exciting opportunity to stand out in the growing world of interactive and immersive gaming. By focusing on targeted audiences with unique needs, preferences, and goals, game developers can create highly engaging and impactful experiences that go beyond traditional gaming.

Why Niche Development Works
- Targeted Audience: Niche markets, such as mindfulness

enthusiasts, neurofeedback trainers, or competitive eSports players, have specific needs that EEG-enabled games can address.
- High Demand for Innovation: EEG technology is still emerging in the gaming industry, meaning there's a growing appetite for creative solutions that combine brainwave control with gaming mechanics.
- Personalized Impact: Games tailored to specific niches allow for deeper immersion, personal growth, or measurable benefits, such as improving focus, mental well-being, or skill development.

Niche Opportunities for EEG and BCI Gaming

Focus and Concentration Games for eSports

Competitive gamers are constantly looking for ways to improve reaction time, focus, and in-game decision-making. EEG-enabled games or tools can help them practice staying in a state of heightened focus, measuring their brain activity as they progress. These tools can also serve as training exercises for professional players.

Mindfulness and Relaxation Games

A growing niche of users is interested in mental health and wellness. EEG-integrated mindfulness games can provide feedback on stress reduction, relaxation, and meditation through brainwave tracking. These games could guide players to achieve calm states or train their minds to stay present.

Educational Brainwave-Controlled Games

For students or children, EEG-enabled games can be designed to teach focus, learning retention, or problem-solving skills. Gamified challenges with real-time brainwave feedback can help learners build cognitive skills while making education more interactive and fun.

Rehabilitation and Neurofeedback Therapy Games

For healthcare-related niches, EEG games can be developed to assist individuals recovering from neurological conditions. Brain-controlled exercises help patients regain cognitive function, improve attention, or manage anxiety in a gamified and motivating way.

Casual BCI-Controlled Fun Games

Brainwave control can also be integrated into casual games for a broader audience. These could be puzzle games, racing games, or relaxation-based experiences where EEG feedback enhances enjoyment or introduces unique game mechanics.

Customizable Games for Self-Improvement
Games tailored for personal growth, such as brain-training applications, allow users to track improvements over time. Players could set their own goals, such as improving focus, lowering stress, or building mental resilience, with EEG metrics guiding progress.

How to Get Started in Niche Game Development

- Start Small: Begin with simple prototypes to test brainwave integration within a specific niche. Tools like Emotiv's API and Muse SDKs make it accessible for indie developers.
- Engage the Community: Collaborate with niche audiences to understand their needs, collect feedback, and refine your game to suit their expectations.
- Focus on Measurable Results: Whether improving focus, achieving relaxation, or enhancing skills, ensure EEG data and game mechanics provide clear, measurable progress for players.
- Monetization Strategies: Consider different models like freemium, subscriptions, or premium game pricing based on the depth and value of the niche solution.

Case Study: A Mindfulness Game

Imagine a game designed to help players meditate effectively. Using EEG, the game monitors brainwaves in real-time, providing immediate feedback on relaxation levels. As players focus and quiet their minds, the game environment could respond—calming music plays, serene visuals appear, and their relaxation "score" increases. Over time, users could measure their progress, improving mindfulness and reducing stress through gamified meditation.

CONCLUSION

Gaming has always been a space where technology and creativity converge, pushing the boundaries of what's possible. With the integration of EEG technology and BCIs, the gaming world stands on the cusp of a new era. From mastering focus and enhancing performance to playing games using only the power of the mind, the potential for innovation is boundless.

In this book, we've explored how EEG technology can transform not just the way we play games but also how we connect with them on a deeper level. Chapter 1 delved into the practical applications of EEG for sharpening focus and improving performance, showcasing how gamers can harness their brainwaves to gain an edge. Chapter 2 opened the door to gaming with the mind through BCIs, an innovation that promises to redefine immersion and interactivity. Chapter 3 took a glimpse into the future, imagining how EEG could revolutionize gaming experiences in the years to come. Finally, Chapter 4 highlighted the exciting opportunities to monetize EEG and gaming, paving the way for entrepreneurs and innovators to create a thriving ecosystem.

Within the exciting intersection of neuroscience, technology, and entertainment, the possibilities are limited only by our imagination. EEG technology has the potential to reshape the gaming industry, fostering greater accessibility, creativity, and personalization. For developers, gamers, and pioneers alike, this is the time to explore, experiment, and innovate.

The future of gaming is not just about faster processors or better graphics; it's about creating experiences that connect us to our very essence—our minds. Whether you're a gamer, a developer, or someone curious about the endless potential of technology, the journey ahead is one of limitless opportunity.

Let the games begin—not just with our hands, but with our minds.

APPENDIX

Templates

Goal Setting and Brainwave Journaling Template
These templates can be copied and reused to track your journey, helping you stay consistent and evaluate progress effectively.

Template 1: Goal Setting
Use this template to set clear, achievable goals for improving focus, performance, or BCI control.

Goal: [What is your specific goal?]
Why is this goal important? [Write your motivation.]

Brainwave Activity: [What brainwave state are you working on – focus, relaxation, etc.?]
Time Commitment: [How many days or weeks will you dedicate to this goal?]

Steps to Achieve the Goal:
1. [Step 1]
2. [Step 2]
3. [Step 3]

Success Measurement: [How will you know you've achieved this goal? Write measurable indicators.]

Template 2: Brainwave Journaling
Track your brainwave activity and progress over time to see how exercises and tools are working for you.

Date: [MM/DD/YYYY]

Activity/Exercise Performed: [Brief description of the activity, e.g., 10-minute focus task]

Brainwave State Observed: [Which brainwave state did you measure – Alpha, Beta, etc.?]

Notes on Experience or Improvement: [Any noticeable changes or improvements, e.g., enhanced focus, reduced stress]

Instructions for Use:
1. Record your activities, exercises, and EEG sessions daily or weekly.
2. Observe changes in your brainwave states and note the outcomes, such as improved focus levels or reduced stress.
3. Use this journal to identify patterns, measure progress over time, and adjust your practices accordingly.

Example Entry

Date: 12/15/2024

Activity/Exercise Performed: 15-minute focus exercise while using Emotiv Insight

Brainwave State Observed: Increased Beta waves

Notes on Experience or Improvement: Felt sharper and more focused during my gaming session immediately afterward.

Frequently Asked Questions (FAQ)

What is EEG, and how does it work?
EEG (Electroencephalography) is a method used to monitor brainwave activity. It measures the electrical signals produced by your brain using non-invasive sensors placed on the scalp. These brainwaves correspond to different mental states such as focus, relaxation, and stress.

Do I need a medical background to use EEG devices?
No, EEG devices like Emotiv Insight and Muse are designed for everyday users without requiring a medical background. This book provides simple, step-by-step instructions to help you understand and use EEG for personal development or gaming.

Can EEG really help improve my gaming performance?
Yes. By understanding your brainwave patterns, you can train yourself to sustain focus, enhance reaction times, and reduce mental fatigue, all of which directly impact gaming performance. Many gamers use EEG tools to monitor and improve their mental state during gameplay.

What are brain-controlled games, and how do they work?
Brain-controlled games, also called BCI games, allow you to control gameplay using your brainwaves. EEG devices detect specific brainwave activity, such as focus or relaxation, and translate it into actions within the game. For example, increasing focus could move a character or object in the game.

What equipment do I need to get started?
You need an EEG headset such as Emotiv Insight or Muse, along with compatible software or apps. These devices are affordable, beginner-friendly, and readily available online.

Is EEG safe to use?
Yes. EEG devices are non-invasive and safe for regular use. They only monitor brainwave activity; they do not emit any signals into

your brain.

How long does it take to see results when using EEG?
It varies depending on consistency and the goals you're working toward. Some users notice improvements in focus or relaxation within a few days, while others may take weeks to see significant changes. Regular practice and tracking progress are key.

Can EEG be used for stress management outside of gaming?
Absolutely. EEG is a powerful tool for stress management. By learning to recognize and control brainwave activity, you can develop techniques for relaxation, mindfulness, and mental clarity.

ABOUT THE AUTHOR

Dr. Niloufar Sarraf

Dr. Niloufar Sarraf holds a PhD in Neuro-Information Science, along with a Bachelor's degree in Cognitive Psychology and Statistics and a Master's degree in Human-Computer Interaction. She received the prestigious Outstanding Doctoral Thesis Award, from Queensland University  of Technology, marking a significant milestone in a long journey of exploring the intersection of human biology, information science, and artificial intelligence. With over a decade of experience working in product research and user research within Silicon Valley's tech industry, Sarraf has developed a deep understanding of how humans and technology interact.

Long before starting her PhD, Sarraf became fascinated with the development of neural networks in AI, particularly with how these artificial systems processed digital inputs. It was during this period, over twelve years ago, that she noticed a striking difference between how artificial systems process information and the complex, analog ways in which biology and the human brain operate. This realization sparked a passion for understanding the deeper nature of information: How is information processed on a biological and atomic level, and why weren't biological systems being used as data inputs in AI?

Driven by these questions, Sarraf embarked on a personal journey of independent postdoctoral research, pursuing answers to why biological intelligence—so rich and intricate within the human body—had not yet been fully integrated into artificial systems. This book is the culmination of years of study, both academic and self-directed, into the potential for merging bioelectrical signals, neural oscillations, and AI systems, offering new insights into the future of technology and intelligence.

BOOKS BY THIS AUTHOR

Neural Oscillations (Brainwaves) Analysis: A Step-By-Step Guide To Collecting And Analyzing Eeg Data With Emotiv Epoc Neuroheadset Series & Eeglab Matlab

This book covers a step-by-step guide on the mechanics of setting up, collecting, processing, and visualizing raw EEG data (brainwaves) using Emotiv EPOC neuroheadset series with the EEGLAB (MATLAB) compiled environment open-source software. The step-by-step guide covered in this volume covers the basic mechanics and is not about complex or one-off EEG cases. This guide is ideal for people who want to get into EEG research, using Emotiv & EEGLAB, but do not know how to start. This guide should work well with all of the EPOC neuroheadset series; the EPOC, EPOC+, as well as EPOCx neuroheadsets. Whether you are a researcher, practitioner, or simply interested in the human brain, you will find it useful to study brainwaves primarily because brain frequencies tend to tell us how humans respond to stimuli at the neurological level. EEG data (brain frequencies or brainwaves) has several benefits compared to other imaging techniques or pure behavioral observations. This manual is the type of step-by-step guide that I wished I had when I was doing my grad studies. If you are interested in human brainwaves and want to learn one particular way of collecting and analyzing raw brain frequencies (EEG data), this volume is for you! By the end of this eBook, you will feel confident and uplifted enough to autonomously collect, analyze, and visualize raw brainwaves (EEG data). You will also feel confident to expand on the scope of this volume and showcase your EEG data analysis.

Neural Oscillations In Neural Networks: Top Neural Networks That Work Best With Eeg Data And Top Eeg Task Classifications And Data Signals That Work Best With Neural Networks

Whether you are a student, an experienced neuroscientist, a computer scientist, or a curious individual, this book is designed to: 1) provide you with an overview of the fundamentals of neural oscillations (EEG or brainwaves), and neural networks (e.g. deep learning), and 2) cover the top deep neural network architectures that work best with neural oscillations/EEG data, top EEG classification tasks that work best with neural networks, and top EEG signals that work best as input data for neural networks. The main aim of this book is to provide you with the fundamentals needed to get you started. Detailed technical and programming specifics of these disciplines are beyond the scope of this book.

Symbiotic Intelligence: When Biological And Artificial Minds Merge: Rethinking Intelligence In The Next Generation Ai And Robotics: Exploring The Fusion Of Biosignals And Artificial Intelligence.

In an era where artificial intelligence is reshaping our world, Symbiotic Intelligence offers an exploration of how the fusion of biological and artificial minds could redefine intelligence as we know it. This thought-provoking body of work delves into the deep relationship between human biosignals—such as brainwaves, heart rates, and other cellular electrical signals—and the next generation of AI and robotics.

Drawing on years of independent postdoctoral work, the author brings fresh insights into how future AI systems could learn from the biosignals that power our bodies, creating machines that don't just mimic humans but become their extensions, enhancing scientific research and offering new perspectives on human biology.

Symbiotic Intelligence examines how feeding in real-time biosignals via wearables and other means can influence machine learning and advance the potential of AI in ways we've only begun to imagine. This book is for anyone interested in the cutting edge of AI, biofeedback technologies, and the speculative future of human-machine interaction. Whether you're a researcher, technologist, or simply curious about how technology might evolve to work with us rather than for us, Symbiotic Intelligence offers a new vision for the role the advanced AI systems (AGI/ASI) can play in the years to come.

Harnessing Brainwaves For Better Living And Success: A Practical Step-By-Step Guide To Using Simple Affordable Eeg And Brainwaves Devices For Stress Relief, Focus, Personal Success And Growth

Unlock the power of your brainwaves and embark on a transformative journey of self-discovery and personal growth—all for less than the cost of a fitness tracker. In Harnessing Brainwaves for Better Living and Success, you'll learn how to use affordable EEG devices like Emotiv and Muse (priced under $300) to explore your mental states, manage stress, enhance focus, and supercharge your personal development practices. This practical, step-by-step guide makes cutting-edge neuroscience accessible to everyone, helping you harness the potential of your own brainwaves to create meaningful change in your life. Whether you're looking to build mindfulness, improve productivity, or gain deeper self-awareness, this book empowers you to take control of your mind and thrive.

www.ingramcontent.com/pod-product-compliance
Lightning Source LLC
Chambersburg PA
CBHW071100240526
45471CB00016B/2281